BEFORE
Marilyn

BEFORE
Marilyn

THE BLUE BOOK MODELING YEARS

ASTRID FRANSE AND
MICHELLE MORGAN

Thomas Dunne Books
St. Martin's Press
New York

For Marilyn Monroe and Emmeline Snively, with much love and thanks.

Astrid: For my mother and my family.

Michelle: For Suzie Kennedy. You will always be 'Blanche' to me. xx

THOMAS DUNNE BOOKS.
An imprint of St. Martin's Press.

www.thomasdunnebooks.com
www.stmartins.com

The Library of Congress Cataloging-in-Publication Data is available upon request

ISBN 978-1-250-08590-0 (hardcover)
ISBN 978-1-250-08591-7 (e-book)

St. Martin's Press books may be purchased for educational, business, or promotional use.
For information on bulk purchases, please contact the Macmillan Corporate and Premium
Sales Department at 1-800-221-7945, extension 5442, or write to
specialmarkets@macmillan.com.

Originally published in Great Britain by The History Press

First U.S. Edition: November 2015

10 9 8 7 6 5 4 3 2 1

CONTENTS

ACKNOWLEDGEMENTS

The authors would like to thank the following people:

Memory Monroe and Marco van der Munnik, who introduced us and planted the seed for this remarkable project. We would also like to thank Marco for providing some photographs from his collection.

Those wonderful people who provided photographs, interviews, information or support for the project, including: Suzanne Van Leendert, Christopher Ryan, Frank Van Osch, Chuck Murphy/ One West Publishing, David Conover Junior, Margaret Miller/ Richard C. Miller Estate, Roland and Chris Hueth, Kim Goodwin, Greg Schreiner, Melinda Mason, Dionne Abraham, Eric Patry, Michael Reynard, Eduardo Caballero, Livia Vidicki, Debra Holden, Annabelle Stanford, Steve Hayes, Bill Pursel, Maria Musikka, The Estate of Joseph Jasgur, Joyce Black, Beverly La Belle, Paul Jordan, Noreen Nash, Paula Knotter, Darren Julien of Julien's Auctions, Matt Butson, Irvin Gelb, Mamie Van Doren, Claartje van Dijk, Fiona Maynard, Eric Woodard, Christina Rice, Tara Hanks, Marijane Gray, Fraser Penny, April VeVea, David Wills, Polly Haas, Laura Wagg, Beth Watson, Christine Mas, Scott Fortner and Andrew Hansford.

Also the Marilyn fans who have supported us, and specifically those who have joined the Blue Book Project Facebook page over the past year and helped us identify and find rare photographs. There are too many members to thank each and every one personally, but you all know who you are!

We would also like to thank our agent, Robert Smith, and publisher, The History Press, for believing in this project and giving us the opportunity to tell Marilyn's Blue Book story.

Finally we would like to say a huge thank you to Emmeline Snively. If she had not kept her files for all those years, this project would never have come to fruition. We are both extremely grateful to her.

Michelle would like to thank:

My family, especially Richard, Daisy, Mum, Dad, Paul, Wendy and Angelina. My friends Claire, Helen and Mandy, and my readers, who have always been so supportive. I can't thank you enough; you all mean the world to me.

Astrid would like to thank:

My mother Miep van Anrooy-Biesthorst, who raised me by herself and died, aged 47. My husband Ben Franse. My sons Sargon Franse and Maroen Franse, and their families. Noor Johnson. My business colleagues at Bennies Fifties, who assisted me: Richard Westdijk, Anais Constandse, Rana Stuivenberg, Jack van der Meulen and Julie Schulting (www.benniesfifties.com/www.fiftiesstore.com).

The front and back cover images have been supplied courtesy of Kim Goodwin.

FOREWORD

Marilyn Monroe is probably the most written about movie celebrity of all time. Countless biographies have delved into her life with varying accuracy. Her difficult childhood, early film success and her eventual stardom are chronicled through endless tomes. But one critical area has been only superficially covered – her years early in her career with the Blue Book Modelling Agency. When Norma Jeane walked through their doors on that fateful day on 2 August 1945 her life would forever change.

So much of what Marilyn learned from the Blue Book Modelling Agency would carry her through her entire life, and literally opened many doors for her that allowed access to a film career. Her blonde hair, unique, quivering smile and famous walk were attributes directly related to her education with the agency and its director Emmeline Snively. Adding to all this was a growing confidence in herself and her abilities to function as a model and eventually an actress. Marilyn was obviously destined for greatness, but this could have been all lost to the world if she had not had this turning point in her life. Miss Snively took her under her wing and nurtured and guided her and believed in her abilities. She also may have been responsible for getting Marilyn her first screen test at Twentieth Century Fox Studios.

The most ironic part is that all of this history might have been lost if not for the concern of Miss Snively to save all of the photos, papers and other articles relating to this time. The eventual loss and recovery of these files provides a fascinating story in itself.

The authors, Astrid Franse and Michelle Morgan, have done extensive and exhaustive research into this relatively unknown area of Marilyn's life, and given us tremendous insight into how Marilyn transformed herself from a simple hometown girl into the world's greatest movie star. The book is loaded with unseen photos of Marilyn from this period, as well as other documents and letters. This is certainly a must-have book for Marilyn fans; at last the complete history of this so important part of Marilyn's life will be filled in. But this is also a book to give hope to anyone who dreams big and strives to achieve a better life. Be prepared to fall in love with this glamorous, sensitive, adorable woman.

Greg Schreiner
President, Marilyn Remembered
www.marilynremembered.org

INTRODUCTION

Twenty years ago, Astrid and Ben Franse were in a vintage store in Los Angeles, buying items for their shop, Bennies Fifties. As they spoke to the shopkeeper, a man walked in with a box in his hands and mumbled something about finding it in a locker. Nobody seemed aware of the exact contents contained inside, but, despite that, the store owner bought the item to sell in his shop. Astrid and Ben overheard the conversation and took an immediate interest in the mysterious contents of the box. They negotiated a deal with the owner and then took the box back home to Europe.

The couple were convinced that what they had just bought was a box of pictures, old newspapers and press clippings mentioning Marilyn Monroe. Thinking the items had probably been collected by a fan, they stored the box under a desk and temporarily forgot about it. In the years ahead Astrid thought often that she should take a good look through to see exactly what was in there, but one year led to another, and before she knew it, two decades had passed and the box remained untouched.

In 2012 – fifty years since the death of Marilyn Monroe – a dealer telephoned from the United States on behalf of a collector, who was interested in buying one of the couple's jukeboxes (a rare 1943 proto-type of the Wurlitzer 1000). During the course of the conversation, he happened to mention that his client was a huge Marilyn Monroe fan, who had previously tried to buy the dress the actress had worn when singing 'Happy Birthday' to President John F. Kennedy. It was at this point that Ben remembered the box under his desk. He told the dealer, and then received a call later that night to say that the Marilyn collector was definitely interested in buying the box.

This information prompted the couple to look at the contents for the very first time. When they lifted the lid, they were absolutely stunned. While Ben and Astrid had always believed the crate held just a series of clippings and memorabilia, they were proved to be wrong. The box actually contained the archives from Miss Emmeline Snively, owner of the Blue Book Modelling Agency, who had signed Marilyn (or Norma Jeane Dougherty as she was then) in 1945.

There were folders containing negatives, letters (one from Marilyn herself), telegrams, agency books, business cards, photos, envelopes, worksheets and much more. There was even a play that had been written by Miss Snively and Joyce Ryan, her secretary, who had once been a Blue Book model. The archive was a monumental discovery and revealed that long after Marilyn's death the agency boss tried to make her memories into a book or documentary, compiling notes and sorting photos along the way. Her efforts went unpublished, however, and eventually she decided to lock her archive away forever.

When news of the discovery hit the newspapers, it caused a sensation. No longer was Astrid the owner of a box of memorabilia; suddenly she was the keeper of a very important piece of history. She decided that, instead of selling the files, she should bring the information to the masses in the form of a documentary and book. As a result, Astrid was inundated with requests from authors, all asking if they could be the one to tell the story of Marilyn's discovery by Emmeline Snively. Their interest was appreciated, but Astrid was determined that she needed to work with someone who understood and respected Marilyn and who would want to fulfil the dreams of Miss Snively just as much as she did herself.

After reading the 2012 biography *Marilyn Monroe: Private and Undisclosed*, Astrid believed that author Michelle Morgan was the best person to write the story. After a successful meeting and many emails back and forth, the two women decided to work together. Their aim? To bring the story of Marilyn's time at the Blue Book Agency to life in a way that only they could: by fusing together the agency archives,

December I5, I953

Dear Miss Lester:

    Intending to do a story on Marilyn Monreo's modeling
school training and first jobs, I have collected sixty
pictures from the photographers who used her as a model
through my efforts. These pictures were captioned to
best tell the story of her modeling career.
    From this group of unpublished pictures I have select-
ed twenty-eight black and white prints, which I feel
would best suit your S.O.P. section. These have been c
contributed by twelve photographers, and are released to
them.They have given me permission to organize and use
them in a model school story. Also I am enclosing six
4 by 5 Kodachrome transparencies - Marilyn's very first
color pictures.
    Of all the write-ups and publicity on this girl no
pictures or stories have been published on her modeling
career,although the modeling has been refered to in
many success stories. As can be readily seen in the
picture of Marilyn's magazine covers, she was a well es
established model in Los Angeles,however her model life
was crammed in to a period of less than two years.
    I want to thank you for sending the most interesting
S.O,P. Book and hope to hear from you shortly.

                              Sincerely yours

                              Emmeline Snively
                                  Director
                              Blue Book Model School

Miss Snively's letter to an editor explaining that the story of Marilyn's modelling career has never been told.
(From the archive of Ben and Astrid Franse)

Astrid's prodigious research into its contents and Michelle's rich knowledge of the actress's life. It was a perfect fit.

From the very beginning, the authors have been adamant that this project should be an extension of what Miss Snively had begun all those years ago. Therefore, this book is not a biography but a unique look into Marilyn's early career in the 1940s and her continuing relationship with the Blue Book Agency. It has also become a tribute not only to Marilyn but to Miss Snively herself, telling the fascinating story of how she played a part in creating a legend. 'If Miss Snively had not been around, there would not have been a Marilyn,' says Astrid. 'She discovered her, she saw her potential.'

Astrid is correct of course. While Marilyn had tentatively begun a modelling career in 1944, her life was to change forever on that fateful day a year later when she walked through the beautiful lobby of the Ambassador Hotel and into the reception of the Blue Book Agency. Emmeline Snively took the young woman under her wing and encouraged her to dye her hair blonde and make several other corrections and adjustments – ultimately helping to launch one of the most successful film careers the world has ever seen.

This book is a tribute to the hard work of both Marilyn Monroe and Emmeline Snively, bringing alive the archives of the agency and reliving a vital part of history: Marilyn Monroe's Blue Book years.

Authors' Note

Miss Snively always referred to her former pupil as Norma Jean Dougherty and later Marilyn Monroe. However, records show that the official spelling of her name was actually Jeane with an 'e'. In order to be factual, the authors have written her name in the official way.

On a similar note, because the agency boss often wrote her notes and letters with business partner Joyce Ryan, she sometimes refers to herself in the third person. Where she did this in the archive, we have – for the most part – kept it that way in the text of the book. The only thing we have changed is where Miss Snively occasionally gets a date incorrect in her notes. These have been corrected to correspond with historical accuracy.

ONE

SPECULATION, UNASSIGNED

Norma Jeane Baker never intended to be a model. Instead she had dreamt of one day becoming an actress, so that she could receive the love so desperately lacking in her childhood. Raised as an orphan, even though both parents were still alive, she was in and out of foster homes and an orphanage until she met a young man called James Dougherty. He was good-looking, sporty and thought of himself as something of a knight in shining armour. She was 15, pretty, scared and desperately looking for a way to avoid another stint in an orphanage. After prompting by her foster mother and future mother-in-law, Norma Jeane reluctantly agreed to marry Dougherty, just weeks after her 16th birthday, and became a teenage housewife.

By 1944 Dougherty had joined the Merchant Marines and Norma Jeane moved in with her in-laws. She found a job at a local defence plant, where she worked first in the typing pool and then on the factory floor, spraying parachutes. The mixture that went into the spray played havoc with the young girl's hair, and she went home each day completely exhausted. She hated the job; she disliked living with her in-laws, but it was wartime and she saw no means of escape. In the end, however, escape found her.

Working for the US government, photographer David Conover found himself visiting the factory to take photos of women working during the war. Spotting Norma Jeane working feverishly at her post, he asked where in the hell she had been hiding, and after explaining that she had just returned from visiting her foster parents, Conover asked if he could take her picture. She whole-heartedly agreed. At that point it seems as though Norma Jeane had been moved from spraying parachutes onto a slightly less dirty job, and the photos taken of her in those next few minutes surely must go down in history as some of the most important.

Wearing a green shirt, grey slacks and her wedding ring, along with a name card firmly attached to her waist band, Norma Jeane posed for Conover, with a broad smile firmly on her face. When she later wrote to her foster aunt Grace, she told her that some of the photographers at the factory that day had also taken moving pictures of her and asked for dates. The girl who had otherwise lived a humdrum, and at times loveless, life must surely have been thrilled by the attention, but she turned down the requests to go out with the photographers. Instead, Norma Jeane concentrated on Conover's professional interest and changed into a red sweater before posing for several more photographs, this time outside the factory environment. Whilst snapping her picture, he asked if she had ever considered modelling. Norma Jeane laughed and assured him that she had not.

David Conover was so impressed with the young factory worker that he returned to her workplace several times to take more shots. Then one morning he called to say that the photos had been developed and had turned out very successfully. Apparently workers at the Eastman Kodak Company asked him, 'Who's your model for goodness sake?' This news pleased Norma Jeane, who remembered the story over ten years later during an interview for the *Bombay Screen* magazine:

> I began to think that maybe he wasn't kidding about how I ought to be a model. Then I found that a girl could make five dollars an hour modelling which was different from working ten hours a day for the kind of money I'd been making at the plane plant.

Conover asked if Norma Jeane would like to travel around Southern California with him; the idea being that she could pose for photographs and learn the correct way to hold herself in front of a camera. She told him she would be happy to go, and after her husband had finished a home visit and returned to the forces, Norma Jeane and Conover put their plans to work. For the next two weeks he snapped her wearing various outfits, including white hot pants teamed with a striped T-shirt, a sweater and a blouse.

While this was the first proper photographic session she had ever taken part in, Norma Jeane was actually no stranger to being in front of a camera and had posed for family and friends on several occasions in the years leading up to the Conover sessions. Her family and friends snapped her standing in front of cars, lying in the grass outside her home and hanging out with teenage pals. She had even been caught on moving camera, strutting confidently on the front lawn while wearing a relative's new fur coat. There was no doubt that from a very early age, Norma Jeane loved the camera and it loved her right back. The time spent on these amateur modelling sessions seem to have put her in good stead, and the Conover photos taken during the first half of 1945 show a young woman poised, professional and, most of all, happy.

'Norma Jeane loved the camera and it loved her right back'

David Conover enjoyed working with Norma Jeane and told his friend Potter Hueth all about her. According to Miss Snively, the former introduced Norma Jeane to the latter with the following words, 'Here's a cute girl who photographs very well. Maybe you can get some work for her.' Hueth liked what he saw, and before long Norma Jeane had posed for him wearing a distinctive striped bikini, which she would also wear later whilst modelling for several photographers, including Joseph Jasgur and Bruno Bernard. Hueth photographed her sitting on a hay bale, which almost landed her in trouble with her husband, who was home at the time. The story goes that while sitting in the barn that day, the young model was asked to remove her wedding ring so that it didn't appear on any of the photos. She did, and accidentally put it down in the hay. By the time the end of the shoot came, the ring was nowhere to be found, and Norma Jeane was forced

Norma Jeane's 'girl-next-door' image shines through in this photograph taken at her home in Los Angeles during the 1940s. (From the collection of Michelle Morgan)

Norma Jeane poses outside a house believed to be that of her foster mother Ana Lower, unknown photographer. (From the collection of Michelle Morgan)

to search through the barn for it. She did not find it at first but luckily discovered it during a second look the next morning.

Through her association with Hueth and Conover, Norma Jeane came into contact with several other photographers, such as Bob Farr and Paul Parry. Both men liked her girl-next-door look but had trouble selling her photographs to magazine editors, who believed she was 'too natural'. Parry later told reporter Jim Henaghan about his first memory of Norma Jeane:

> I was sitting in my office chinning with a couple of other fellows one day, when this girl came in and asked if I thought she could be a model. I'll never forget it because she was wearing a pink sweater – and the other two fellows just fell right off their chairs. Could she!

One of Parry's photographs eventually led to a calendar advertising Mission Orange Drink, which was published in 1952, after Norma Jeane had become a star. One that appeared much sooner, however, came when she teamed up with William Carroll, a photographer looking for a young model to appear on counter displays to advertise his Ansco Color film processing shop. Norma Jeane liked the idea and headed to the beach with Carroll, where a variety of colour shots were taken.

Back at home, the young woman continued to resent being married at such an early age and most certainly did not like having to live under the scrutiny of her husband's family while he was away. Although James Dougherty said initially that he approved of the modelling work – thinking it far easier than working in the factory – he also made it especially clear that he would only tolerate it until he returned from war. After that he was determined that the two would settle down to a normal life with a house and children like every other 'normal' couple. His parents were of the opinion that this should happen too, but they could also see that this was not something on Norma Jeane's mind. As a result, they quickly became worried for their son's future.

'Although James Dougherty initially approved of the modelling work ... he made it especially clear that he would only tolerate it until he returned from war'

At this point, it would seem that she was being faithful to Dougherty, and remained so for some time after becoming a model. Sister-in-law Elyda Nelson later recalled that while Norma Jeane was aware that other wives dated while their men were away, she never commented or gossiped about such things and instead just ignored the activity and got on with her own life. Norma Jeane later backed this up when talking about her own experience of dealing with unwanted male attention:

> I didn't have much trouble brushing them off. I found that if I just looked sort of stupid, or pretended I didn't know what they were talking about, they soon gave up in disgust. Some wolves are sinister, others are just good time Charlies trying to get something for nothing. Others make a game of it. The last type is most interesting.

Enjoying a company day out at the Radioplane picnic, unknown photographer. (From the archive of Ben and Astrid Franse)

Norma Jeane and her colleagues have fun at the Radioplane picnic. Unkown photographer. (From the collection of Michelle Morgan)

Her attitude towards the wolves of Hollywood was also demonstrated when William Carroll initially rang to introduce himself before their photograph session. She refused to have anything to do with him, until he assured her that he was a professional, known to Conover and Hueth, and interested in taking her photo, nothing else. Bill Burnside, who met her in 1946, had the same kind of experience: 'Physically she was wary of men and was wary of me for the first months of our knowing each other.'

Despite this, Norma Jeane's in-laws continued to worry about her future as a married woman. While she had worked at the munitions factory the family had trusted her completely, possibly because mother-in-law Ethel worked there too and could keep an eye on her, but also because the men there were considered 'ordinary Joes' who could be brushed off without a moment's thought. Everyone recognised how beautiful she was, however, and at one point, Norma Jeane was even crowned 'Queen of the Radio Plane Picnic' during a company outing. The family had been happy with the achievement, but now everything had changed and her in-laws were more than a little concerned.

In hindsight, it is easy to understand why the family were concerned about Norma Jeane's new-found interest, especially when it came to going around town with various photographers that were not known to the family. Most of those who worked in Hollywood were gentlemen, as confirmed by fellow starlet and model Annabelle Stanford. She insists that no matter what she was modelling – whether it be negligees, swimming costumes or underwear – there were never any passes made towards her and everyone conducted themselves in a professional, decent manner. However, there were certainly several photographers who were known in the industry as being less than perfect or discreet, and the models saw to it that they were always on guard in their presence. One such man was known to some of the women as 'a pig' because of his uncouth behaviour, and he often became so aroused by the bikini-clad girls in his presence that his physical excitement could not be disguised.

In 1940's Hollywood there was also the issue of the casting couch, which could become a big problem for any girl wishing to turn their

Hollywood as it looked in 1945, when Norma Jeane signed with the Blue Book Agency. (From the collection of Michelle Morgan)

modelling careers into acting ones. This is apparent with the story of one model, who arrived at a film studio only to find herself being shuttled towards a bed, discreetly kept in a room joined to the casting director's office. Calling her 'Cutie Pie', the man tried to convince the young woman that if she slept with him, he would ensure she got acting jobs every single day of her career. She was married and told him very firmly that if he forced her into doing such a thing, she would detest him forever and never be anything but an enemy to him. Astonishingly, the director became very embarrassed by her response. 'I have never been told off so politely,' he told her, and vowed never to try it on with her again. Surprisingly, he cast her in a movie anyway, and he kept his promise of keeping his hands to himself.

Although she was still new to the modelling game, Norma Jeane quickly became aware of what went on behind closed doors in some of the studios – both photographic and movie. She was so determined not to get herself into a sticky situation that she would often drive herself to and from modelling appointments in her husband's car. That way she would not fall into the trap of a photographer insisting on giving her a lift home after the shoot and taking his chances in a quiet, deserted lane. 'She would hold up her key ring, jingle it and say cutely, "I've got my own transportation",' Miss Snively later wrote.

Norma Jeane leaning against an open-top car, unknown photographer. (From the collection of Debra Holden)

'She would hold up her key ring, jingle it and say cutely, "I've got my own transportation"'

This still didn't please her in-laws, however, and things came to a head one evening when Norma Jeane was driving home from a modelling job and, by her own admission, was 'dreaming again'. Before she knew it, a car appeared in front of her and she was unable to stop, crashing head-on into the vehicle and writing off Jim's car in the process. 'All I have is a small bump on the head,' she told her sister-in-law, 'But you should see our poor car, it's completely demolished.'

It would seem that the car incident was the beginning of the end between Norma Jeane and the Dougherty family because, not long after, she decided enough was enough and moved into the home of former foster parent 'Aunt' Ana Lower. This was a huge step. Not only did she now have some kind of independence, but she knew that by distancing herself from her in-laws the gap between herself and James Dougherty would be widened too. The long-distance marriage would struggle on for another year, but the end was most certainly looming.

'Here was a child who had rarely felt loved before, though the camera seemed to adore her'

While modelling might have caused problems between Norma Jeane and her husband's family, she was still determined that it would be her key to a better future for herself. Here was a child who had rarely felt loved before, though the camera seemed to adore her. The happiness is clear to imagine, even though there were many times when Norma Jeane had to work initially for free. The reason for this was that if the photographer could not sell his work, then he would not be paid, and in turn she wouldn't be either.

Norma Jeane had first agreed to work this way with photographer Potter Hueth, doing what Miss Snively described as 'Speculation, Unassigned'. However, after a time she began to think seriously about her future, and so spoke to Hueth about what she could do to make her career all the more successful and worthwhile. He told Norma Jeane about an agency located in the Ambassador Hotel that was always on the lookout for girls with a talent before the camera. She liked what she heard, and in early August 1945 she travelled with Hueth from her home in West Los Angeles all the way to Wilshire Boulevard so that she could be introduced to Miss Emmeline Snively, owner of the Blue Book Modelling Agency.

Opposite: Beautiful early portrait of Norma Jeane, complete with a mass of brunette curls. Unknown photographer. (From the collection of Eduardo Caballero)

TWO

NO. 37, CASINO FLOOR

*E*mmeline Snively was born on 2 May 1909 to Myrtle and Frank Snively. An only child, she spent much of her childhood in Ohio and Iowa, where her father worked in newspaper advertising. By 1930 Frank had passed away and Myrtle and Emmeline were trying their luck in Los Angeles: Mrs Snively as a boarding house manager and her daughter as an art student at Holmby College and later UCLA. Photos taken during her time at college show Miss Snively as a delicate-featured young woman, often unsmiling and somewhat serious. Still, her skill and poise in front of a camera is everywhere apparent, and this expertise was to come in very useful in the years ahead.

After graduating in 1934, Miss Snively began teaching art, but over the course of several years she became more interested in the other jobs Hollywood had to offer. An intelligent woman, she could see that there was a large amount of young people desperate to get past the studio gates to seek fame and fortune – in all likelihood she probably saw examples of this every day during her classes. Miss Snively's mind began to wander, and, after much thought, she took the brave decision to leave the sensible land of teaching behind and go into the trickier – but more lucrative – modelling world.

*Miss Emmeline Snively,
head of the Blue Book
Agency. Unkown
photographer. (From
the archive of Ben and
Astrid Franse)*

Unlike most young women interested in the profession, Miss Snively wasn't planning to pose for photographers herself. Instead she decided that there was a real need and gap in the market for a model school, a place to show girls how they too could make a living in the industry. In the late 1930s she found an ideal space in Westwood Village and launched her agency as the Village School. '[I] specialized in training girls for photographic and fashion modelling,' she later wrote in her brochure. 'Graduates have progressed into many fields of fashion, photography and entertainment ... Many have been claimed by the Motion Picture Studios.'

Very soon Miss Snively began enrolling young women onto her 'Blue Book': a catalogue she published every year that featured models available for hire. She also started teaching them everything they could ever wish to know about the finer points of modelling. 'The school offers a non-professional course featuring charm, posture, figure control, wardrobe building and personal development,' she wrote.

'The school offers a non-professional course featuring charm, posture, figure control, wardrobe building and personal development'

By the early 1940s Miss Snively had moved her establishment into a building on Sunset Boulevard, next door to the famous Bublichki restaurant. While there, she found a way of publicising the business in the shape of beauty contests to find Miss May, Miss Summer and any other Miss she could think of. One lady who won Miss November 1943 was Frances Adolf, an 18 year old who took great delight in showing off her large trophy while talking about her budding law career. Another lucky winner was 19-year-old Tyra Vaughn, who won the Miss Spring 1944 competition and posed happily for reporters, who dubbed her a press agent's dream.

The contests were so popular that they continued to run for years. Miss Snively wrote about them in the 1960 edition of her Blue Book catalogue and included photos of the popular event:

At the opening of the new Los Angeles Sports Arena ... for the Do It Yourself Show, fifty Blue Book Models produced the complete beauty contest. Famous judges were Earl Leaf, magazine

photographer; Pamela Ann Searle, Miss England; Dick Sargent, actor; Earl Moran, calendar artist, and master photographer, Max Munn Autrey.

As well as these contacts, she also made herself available as a judge at numerous events, such as a special Miss Catalina contest that was held in June 1956.

Back in the early days, word quickly spread about the agency, and Miss Snively took the opportunity of sharing her thoughts and beauty tips with several different authors. The subsequent articles were then syndicated around the United States, bringing even more attention to the venture. One such piece was written by features writer Sam Jackson and showed a photograph of the agency boss taking notes whilst on a telephone – the backdrop being a wall full of photos of glamorous young women. In the article Miss Snively stated that at least 10,000 girls had walked through her doors, and while this was possibly a slight exaggeration, it is true to say that the company was gathering steam at a monumental rate. It became such a success that the time came when Miss Snively decided to pack up her portfolio, covers, notes and files, and move to an even bigger and better office. 'For your convenience, the school has been moved into a more central location, the Ambassador Hotel, and the name changed to The BLUE BOOK School,' she wrote.

Opened at midnight on 1 January 1921, the Ambassador was legendary for its Cocoanut Grove night club and the beautiful people who swanned through its doors. From the very beginning it promised to be a place of grandeur and fascination, with 27 acres of

Opposite: An animated Miss Snively shows off her famous wall of magazine covers. Unkown photographer. (From the archive of Ben and Astrid Franse)

This photograph of the Ambassador Hotel was taken in August 1945 – the month Norma Jeane walked into the Blue Book Agency for the first time. Unknown photographer. (From the collection of Michelle Morgan)

This Kurt Teich postcard shows the pool area of the Ambassador Hotel. Miss Snively used this location many times for her models. (From the collection of Michelle Morgan)

luxurious gardens, palm trees, a beautiful pool and every luxury a guest could possibly need. On the very day the doors swung open for the first time, the hotel boasted a roster of 500 staff, some of whom had previously worked for empresses and dukes, and many who had moved from all over the world just so they could work at the prestigious establishment.

The hotel included a ballroom big enough for 1,000 dancing couples, a theatre, a bank, many guest bedrooms and vast dining rooms. Orchestras played while patrons ate their lunch and dinner, and every weekend the same ensemble would entertain groups of guests in the hotel lobby. For those requiring physical activity, a golf course was situated just down the road, and a riding school was also in operation nearby. Children weren't left out either, and the pool was a magnet for families from the very beginning, as was the porch full of parrots, where youngsters could often be found talking to the colourful birds that lived there. There was also a vast array of goldfish bowls, art nouveau paintings, ornaments and leather-bound registers, all of which made the Ambassador a winner for young and old alike.

On the day the doors opened for the very first time, thousands of people crammed into the hotel to register from as far away as London to take a peek inside the sprawling building. Cars crowded outside to such a degree that they caused congestion and hold-ups around the block, while white-gloved bellboys showed guests to their rooms and made sure everyone felt like a star. As could be expected, the opulence of the hotel was a magnet for real-life movie stars too, as well as directors, producers and all manner of other film-related clientele. Actress Carole Lombard won dance competitions there in her days before stardom and then dined frequently after that; Rudolf Valentino was known to do a mean Charleston round the dance floor; and movie comedienne Thelma Todd took part in various charity events and parties throughout her career.

'white-gloved bellboys showed guests to their rooms and made sure everyone felt like a star'

By the mid-1940s many of the stars that had graced the Ambassador with their presence (including the three mentioned above) had passed away, though the hotel was still considered to be one of the most fabulous in Los Angeles. People continued to travel from all over the world to stay in its famed rooms or star-spot in the Cocoanut Grove, and holiday makers would often buy the Curt Teich postcards available in the lobby, sending home scrawling notes to envious family members about the magnificent view from their windows. When it came to spending time at the hotel, and in particular its famed nightclub, Norma Jeane Dougherty was no exception. While she was most certainly not a regular there, the girl had some treasured memories of visiting with her mother and foster aunt during the 1930s, and by the mid-1940s she had enjoyed some rare but elaborate evenings out with her husband, James.

When it opened in January 1944, Emmeline Snively's agency was a welcome addition to the Ambassador, occupying No. 37, Casino Floor – a store previously assigned to an organisation offering entertainment classes in exchange for buying war stamps. Blue Book joined a mix of forty already established shops – including clothes stores, a hairdresser and various other retail outlets – and was also in close proximity to the Steinie Photographic Studio. In the years ahead, Miss Snively would often use the proprietor, Erwin Steinmeyer, to make test shots of the girls on her books, including Norma Jeane.

Two examples of the kind of postcards guests could expect to find in the lobby of the Ambassador Hotel. (From the archive of Ben and Astrid Franse)

Once installed in her new office, Miss Snively covered the walls of the reception in glossy photos of her clients past and present, just as she had done in the previous building. She then enjoyed pointing out the models' achievements to all who came into the agency on business. In her office there were photos too, along with a statue of Nefertiti, which stood on her desk. 'She was the most beautiful woman of her era,' Miss Snively told actor Steve Hayes and explained that she kept it to show young girls that beauty was not a new thing.

'she kept it to show young girls that beauty was not a new thing'

New promotional materials were prepared that encouraged prospective photographers and models to 'stop in and see the new quarters'. Existing models were photographed getting ready under the watchful eye of Miss Snively and what appears to be her mother. They were then snapped helping to pin the new sign to the wall and talking with the boss about future work opportunities. Miss Snively also made sure she was photographed – wearing her finest clothes – at the front of the hotel, talking to one of her prettier girls.

By this time a new publicity gimmick had occurred to her. Always astute and forward thinking, Miss Snively ordered a specially made life ring with the words 'Blue Book Models Hollywood' printed onto it. Over the coming years the agency boss would ask several photographers to travel to a variety of locations, such as the Ambassador Hotel gardens and Santa Monica beach, with

A model poses next to the Blue Book signage in the Ambassador Hotel, in a brochure for the Blue Book Agency. (From the archive of Ben and Astrid Franse)

Left: Miss Snively shows as much sophistication as her model in this photo from the Blue Book brochure. The picture was taken in the grounds of the Ambassador Hotel. (From the archive of Ben and Astrid Franse)

Below: Miss Snively interviews a prospective client in another photo from the Blue Book brochure. (From the archive of Ben and Astrid Franse)

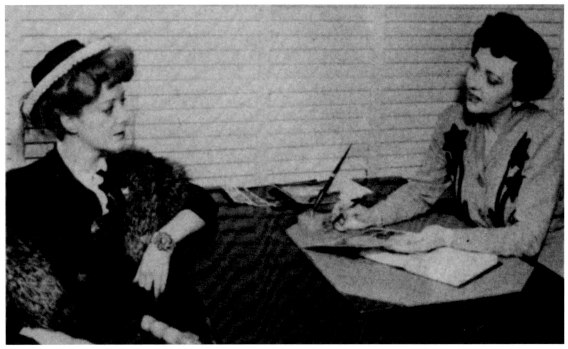

some of her girls. There they would snap the models posing and playing with the prop and the results would go into brochures and adverts for the agency, as well as hang in the reception for visitors to admire.

Miss Snively had firmly established herself as a 'grand dame' agency boss, and when her mother Myrtle joined the business they became something of a powerhouse, running the agency like a well-oiled machine. From her notes and memories, it is clear to see that Miss Snively cared very much for the women who worked there and was always on hand to dish out advice wherever needed. Sitting the women down, she would encourage all of them to never think of modelling as a full-time career. Instead, she said, they should look to the future, to see posing for photographers as a bridge to better things, such as lucrative jobs in Hollywood studios or even the theatre.

While Miss Snively was encouraging to those already working for her, she was still picky about whom she signed on to her

Blue Book advert 'Let me work for you' with a Blue Book model posing with the life ring, photographer: Joseph Jasgur. (From the archive of Ben and Astrid Franse. Reproduced with permission from the Joseph Jasgur Estate)

famous blue book, choosing only to take on those she thought could achieve a fair amount of photographic assignments. After all, she was paid commission from jobs they obtained, so if they did not earn anything, neither did she. Any prospective girls had to fill out a form, giving their name, address, age, height and weight. Additionally she would ask for measurements of bust, waist and hips, along with the colour of hair, skin and eyes. Two snapshots were required: a bathing-suit shot and a portrait.

If the photos grabbed Miss Snively's attention, she would then ask the girls to come along for an interview. There she endeavoured to make sure the models had five different qualities: good temperament, good health, good face, good figure and 'adequate training

Secretary Joyce Ryan talks to models in the Blue Book reception. Photographer: possibly Joe Jasgur. (From the collection of Christopher Ryan)

in make-up, hair styling, posing and taking camera direction'. The former points were all up to the model to obtain; the latter could be taught at the modelling school.

Actor Steve Hayes met both Miss Snively and her mother in the 1950s. Myrtle, he said, was very severe in manner, but Miss Snively was 'attractive, with bright, sparkly eyes; very well groomed with jewellery, nice clothes and pearls'. So as to gain respect from the photographers and the models on her books, the agency boss spent a long time perfecting her look and was always elegant, with her hair immaculately styled. She was not beautiful in a conventional way, but she paid attention to little details and was rarely seen without nail polish, a smart suit and small hat.

Opposite: Unknown 1940s model with life ring. Photographer: possibly Joseph Jasgur. (From the archive of Ben and Astrid Franse. Reproduced with permission from the Joseph Jasgur Estate)

In conversation, Miss Snively could be very quick-witted and hold her own, no matter whom she was talking to or where the conversation led. She could be fun and light-hearted but was no pushover. Her company came before everything, and while she was not averse to going on dates occasionally, she was not prepared to give up anything she had achieved in exchange for a steady relationship. As a result Miss Snively never married and spent her entire life as a single woman. That said, she was no stranger to the odd date, and rumours abound that at one point she was involved with a successful businessman. Flirting came easy too, and she even managed to do so in her many letters to magazines. To Vincent T. Tajiri, one of the editors of *Art Photography* magazine, she wrote, 'Thank you for your patience and I hope all goes well. Our mutual friend, Earl Leaf is back among the Hollywood beauties. I understand a beard provokes even more admiration in the east than it does here. Why is that do you know?' The editor replied favourably, by writing, 'Call me Vince and I'll follow with Emmy.'

'Emmeline could be very quick-witted and hold her own no matter whom she was talking to'

To cement the idea that they were powerful women, both Miss Snively and her mother spent a great deal of time changing themselves from 'normal' Americans into high-class Englishwomen. Quite bizarrely, this involved telling business associates that they had moved to California from the United Kingdom. This was a rather eccentric move on their part and resulted in both Myrtle and Emmeline speaking in fake British accents. This has confused biographers and people who knew them to this very day.

'She spoke in a nasal, high-pitched voice,' remembers Steve Hayes. 'Spoke very well but very rapidly.' Steve – an Englishman himself – never commented on the accent because he was hoping that one day she may want to represent him and didn't wish to insult her. However, it was very apparent to him and others that she was putting on 'airs' and that the Englishness in her persona was, to all intents and purposes, fake.

Certainly neither Emmeline or Myrtle were known to speak that way in front of people who knew them before their success; nor did they speak with an accent in front of their family. By 1962, when Miss Snively was interviewed about Marilyn's death, the inflection was certainly gone, but in the 1940s she prided herself on her 'Englishness'. Why the two women felt the need to speak with a British accent is up for debate, and it seems that nobody ever enquired as to why they were doing it. However, one reason could be that they felt it provided the agency with a certain amount of respectability and decorum. This was to be important, considering a possible side of the business which some may say was not particularly upright.

With the agency being located in the hugely popular Ambassador Hotel, it became a magnet for businessmen looking for someone to accompany them to the various entertainment venues on site. Miss Snively evidently saw an opportunity, and by many accounts she grabbed it with both hands. During research for this book, a variety of people who knew the agency during the 1940s and 1950s have commented that while there were certainly a great deal of full-time models on the books, others were taking on work as dates and escorts to make extra money.

'It was really an escort service from which lonely businessmen could employ a young woman to dine with,' said one person who knew the agency in 1945. 'The LAPD maintained a close watch.' A former 1940's model further explained that the Blue Book Agency

The
BLUE BOOK
SCHOOL
of
Photographic
and
Fashion Modeling
Established 1939

Grooming for:

Photographic & Fashion Modeling

Motion Pictures

Character Development

Success & Beauty

Ambassador Hotel   DRexel 7316

124

Advertisement for the Blue Book School. (From the archive of Ben and Astrid Franse)

was known to expect certain 'social responsibilities and social efforts from the girls there. None of the agencies I worked with did that, but there was a definite rumour that Blue Book was a house of mischief and I wanted nothing to do with it.'

It would appear that for the most part the women interested in taking on the escort work were those who perhaps weren't earning enough money to support themselves through modelling alone. These young women would not only subsidise their work by going out with men at the hotel, but also by working the Hollywood party scene, attending events with various men-about-town. It should be noted that there is no proof that the girls' jobs ever went any further than accompanying their dates to various night-clubs and restaurants, and Miss Snively makes absolutely no mention of anything untoward in her notes. Instead, if the rumours are true, she kept this side of her business firmly under wraps, though did hint at it briefly during a later interview: 'Many of my other girls whose husbands were overseas, dated on several nights of the week. But not Norma Jeane.'

'there was a definite rumour that Blue Book was a house of mischief'

Her comments bring us to the subject of whether or not Norma Jeane took advantage of the extra money available for dating jobs, once she too had signed with the agency. It should be stressed that no one interviewed for this book ever believed that it was possible for the young woman to be involved in any way whatsoever. In fact everyone expressed the exact opposite opinion, stating that Norma Jeane was never the kind of girl who would have got herself embroiled in any kind of activity outside the agency.

This is further emphasised by the fact that the young model was never known to be particularly well off and did not dress or behave like someone who had any degree of disposable income. Indeed, one friend remembers that for a short time, between modelling jobs, Norma Jeane even took a temporary office post at the Pan Pacific Auditorium, just to make ends meet. It was a short-lived position, designed only to get her out of a tight situation financially, but shows that if the model were prepared to work a temporary clerical job then she certainly would have shown no interest in making an easy buck as a Blue Book escort.

Opposite: Blue Book models in the agency office. The man sitting at the desk is believed to be artist Earl Moran. Photographer: Earl Leaf (From the archive of Ben and Astrid Franse)

Models are joined by Miss Snively as they look through their latest photographs. Photographer: Earl Leaf. (From the archive of Ben and Astrid Franse)

Miss Snively sits in her own car, which sports Blue Book signage. Her models pose next to her. Photographer: Earl Leaf.
(From the archive of Ben and Astrid Franse)

Miss Snively enjoys a joke with her models and Earl Moran. Photographer: Earl Leaf. (From the archive of Ben and Astrid Franse)

Miss Snively poses once again in her car, while her models enjoy a joke. Photographer: Earl Leaf. (From the archive of Ben and Astrid Franse)

Norma Jeane later spoke about an episode that happened while she was modelling, which emphasises the fact that she was definitely not for sale and that Miss Snively tried hard to keep her from that kind of exposure:

When I was modelling I did mostly play clothes and bathing suits. I used to meet a lot of wolves among the buyers who wanted to take me to dinner and give me trinkets, but I always told them the agency people were very strict and wouldn't let me go out with anyone I met during business hours.

Miss Snively's decision to allow some of the girls to go out on dates with hotel guests had a definite downside. Models in the area heard rumours of the other side of the business and were told by their own modelling agencies to stay away. Mary Webb Davis had created her agency several years before Miss Snively did, and she very quickly became one of the most influential women in the business. She was known to be a tough, no-nonsense woman, smoker of unfiltered cigarettes, wearer of huge eyelashes, and undeniably chic and fashionable. Davis always spoke her mind and could be rather intimidating at times, but she was excellent at her job, gaining her high-class fashion models so much work that she became one of the most respected women in Hollywood. 'Some people can play the violin, others can cook. My talent is my photographic eye,' she said in 1961. 'I can pick the one girl from fifty who will be a success.'

'I can pick the one girl from fifty who will be a success'

One model who worked for Webb Davis in the 1940s remembers that the girls were encouraged to stay away from Blue Book, avoid working at the Ambassador wherever possible and instead take part in fashion shows and shoots at the Biltmore or Beverly Hills Hotel. These establishments, Webb felt, were far more prestigious and high standing, and ideal places for models to show off their skills. 'The Mary Webb Davis Agency was very decent, very popular,' remembered client Annabelle Stanford. 'It was very strict, structured and had no nonsense at all. There were lots of designers all around and many glamorous outfits to model. I never got asked to go out with any of the people I worked with.'

Opposite: Earl Moran spends time with four of the Blue Book models. Photographer: Earl Leaf. (From the archive of Ben and Astrid Franse)

THREE

FAME HAS A WAY

'Out of the dozens of girls that attend modelling school and enter the modelling profession, a few have the qualifications to make them cover girls,' wrote Emmeline Snively in the 1950s. So it would be true to say that Miss Snively, who had seen every kind of girl the profession had to offer, did not think there was anything too out-of-the-ordinary about the girl standing in her office at the Ambassador Hotel on 2 August 1945. She noted in her file:

> Norma Jeane had been brought to the hotel by photographer Potter Hueth, wearing a simple white dress and armed with her modelling portfolio, which actually offered no more than a few choice snaps … You wouldn't necessarily wear a white dress on a modelling job, and it was as clean and white and ironed and shining as she was.

In the archive, Miss Snively made extensive notes about the meeting and spoke about it frequently from that moment on. From her memories and quotes, we can piece together a snippet of what happened during that momentous afternoon on the Casino Floor of the Ambassador Hotel …

Hueth introduced the young woman to the agency boss and spread out the few photographs in front of her, one of which Miss Snively had apparently seen prior to the meeting. However, while she was

busy looking at Norma Jeane, the girl herself was more interested in staring at the magazine covers and publicity photos gracing the walls.

'Those are the prettiest girls I have ever seen,' she muttered, almost to herself, before turning to Miss Snively. 'Do you think I could ever get my picture on a magazine cover?'

Miss Snively looked her up and down. 'Of course,' she smiled. 'You're a natural.'

She then sat down to interview Norma Jeane and noted her statistics on an agency card: 'Size 12, height 5.6, 36 bust, 24 waist, 34 hips. Blue eyes, perfect teeth and blonde, curly hair.'

'Actually,' she later wrote, 'her hair was dirty blonde. California blonde which means that it is dark in the winter and light in the summer. I recall that it curled very close to her head, and was quite unmanageable. I knew at once that it would have to be bleached and worked on.'

'Do you sing?' Miss Snively asked.

'Just a little, that's all,' replied Norma Jeane.

Notes made by Miss Snively about Norma Jeane, including some from 2 August 1945, which was the day Marilyn signed her modelling contract. (From the archive of Ben and Astrid Franse)

'Dance?'

'A little.'

'Ambitions of becoming an actress?'

'No, none at all,' the girl replied.

'How old are you? 17? 18?'

'I'm 20,' Norma Jeane said, though in reality she had only just turned 19.

It is unclear why the young girl felt the need to change her age, but perhaps she felt that if she admitted being a teenager, she would not be signed. She shouldn't have worried, however, as by that time Miss Snively was frequently signing children and teenagers to her school and agency. In 1960 she wrote:

Children from four to twelve appeared in a formal fashion showing at the Ambassador Hotel's famous Embassy Room. Children appear on television and learn to do their own commentary ... Teenagers comprise a large portion of those in the training department, as well as the agency of Blue Book Model Studios. Girls prepare themselves for careers in the fashion field or part time photographic modelling. Classes are scheduled either daytime or evening. Many Blue Book graduates have succeeded in fashion careers. Many others have appeared on National magazine covers and won recognition in beauty contests.

Photographs taken around the time Norma Jeane strolled into the agency show Miss Snively chatting animatedly to mothers and children in her office, while others show the infants themselves gazing up at the famed wall of magazine covers.

'Do you have your own wardrobe?' Miss Snively asked.

'Not really,' Norma Jeane replied. 'I have a few items but not many.'

Miss Snively later recalled, 'I remember she had one white dress with a green yoke [likely the one she had worn in the interview] which looked terrific on her, although models usually shy away from white clothes. It accentuated her bust and called attention to her figure. It was extremely tight across the front.' The only other things she seemed to own were a bathing suit and a teal-blue suit 'that didn't do a thing for her', according to Miss Snively.

Opposite: The Models Bluebook brochure for 1945–46. (From the archive of Ben and Astrid Franse)

'Don't laugh now,' she wrote. 'What she had was a "girl next door" look. All right so you never saw a girl next door who looked like Marilyn Monroe, but that's how she looked the day she came in. And for me at least, that's how she always looked.'

Having looked over the young lady sitting before her, Miss Snively noted that Norma Jeane seemed very surprised to be in the Ambassador Hotel. She had of course been there before, but never in such an exciting capacity. This was truly new and refreshing. 'She kept glancing around at things, out of the corner of her eye,' Miss Snively later told reporter Ted Thackrey. 'Like it was a new world.'

Miss Snively told Norma Jeane that a full-page photograph in the Blue Book models catalogue would cost her $25, and if she wanted to attend a three-month modelling course that would be another $100. The girl's face fell, as there was simply no way she could afford to pay such a huge amount of money, and even if she could, her husband would never agree to their money being paid towards such 'frivolous' adventures.

Noticing the depressed look on the model's face, Miss Snively soon took pity on her and decided that she could pay off the fee from the money made during her future modelling jobs. Norma Jeane sat up and smiled. 'She was so naïve, so sweet and so eager to succeed that my heart went out to her at once,' the agency boss wrote.

'Are you single?' asked Miss Snively.

Norma Jeane no doubt looked uncomfortable to be faced with such a query. 'No, I'm married,' she told the surprised woman, who then wrote the information down on the registration card. This revelation was Miss Snively's worst nightmare, as she later observed in her agency file: 'How to choose a model …. It may be a surprise to some of you that models come in a complete package with mother, father, sister, brother, and worse luck, sometimes even with husband and baby.'

While Norma Jeane may not have come to the agency with a baby (or mother, father, sister or brother for that matter), she most certainly had a husband in the shadows, and this put her behind the other girls right from the very beginning.

'She was so naïve, so sweet and so eager to succeed that my heart went out to her at once'

Miss Snively's school taught young hopefuls all they needed to know about the modelling profession. Photographer: Earl Leaf. (From the archive of Ben and Astrid Franse)

'We at Blue Book Models never entered Marilyn into a beauty contest,' wrote Miss Snively in 1954. 'Because although I thought she was excellent material, she was married at this time. Many of the other students won gifts, trips and recognition that would have taken years to acquire any other way. Being married disqualified her at the outset so she was denied the extra boost that participating in beauty contests might have given her.'

But contests or not, Norma Jeane was determined to make a success of the opportunity she had been given, and after signing with the agency, she entered into her new career and modelling course with great gusto. In typed papers in the archive, the purpose of the 'Visual Grooming and Professional Presentation Course' is described in some detail, with the three main aspects being grooming, presentation and coordination.

First came grooming, which taught the girls how to assess their type, how to dress the part, live the life of a model and make a good first impression. Added to that they were also shown how to select a good wardrobe (essential for Norma Jeane), choose the right colours and make sure the face always had a pleasing expression.

Notes from the Blue Book modelling course. (From the archive of Ben and Astrid Franse)

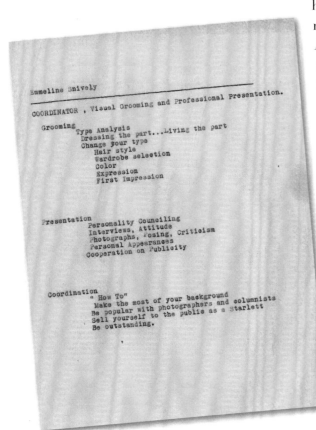

Next was presentation, which gave the models the opportunity of taking part in and learning about personality counselling, mock interviews, attitude training, posing for photographs, dealing with personal appearances, cooperating with publicity and, most importantly, dealing with criticism. For someone as sensitive as Norma Jeane, this aspect of the course would be crucial, though it is questionable as to whether or not she ever really got used to being criticised in her later life and career.

The third aspect of the course was coordination, which showed the models 'how to make the most of your background; how to be popular with photographers and columnists; how to sell yourself to the public as a starlet; and how to be outstanding.' This part of the program must really have caught Norma Jeane's imagination because for the rest of her life she would almost always have time for reporters, even when she really didn't have any need to. This openness led to columnists from all over the world championing her cause and some – such as Louella Parsons and Donald Zec – becoming quite good friends.

An advertising document in the archive reveals more about the lessons and aim of the school:

Blue Book Model students are chosen for their photographic qualities, talent and specialised training. The demand today is for wholesome and intelligent girls. They may be beautiful, but it is more important that they have the quality of distinction.

A course is offered in Photographic Modelling, which requires some previous training in dancing and dramatics. This course prepares girls to model for photographers, illustrators, advertisers, artists and commercial motion pictures.

The course in Fashion Modelling includes many of those things so helpful in everyday living [such] as: personal analysis and improvement, walking, sitting, entering a room, make-up, hair styling and wardrobe selection, besides the actual training in showing clothes.

With the fashion and photographic centre swinging toward the west coast, there are more opportunities for work in this field and more training and organisation is necessary on the part of the models.

Actual experience is offered in Fashion and Photographic Modelling. Most of the students have had the opportunity to do a pay job before graduation.

It is the aim and privilege of the Blue Book Model organisation to help select, organise and promote newcomers on their way to careers in modelling, the theatre and motion pictures.

Evening classes have been arranged for those who are employed… Residence Hall provided for out-of-town girls.

Norma Jeane's first official assignment for Blue Book was as a hostess at an industry show. Unknown photographer.
(Michael Reynard collection. Property of Michael Reynard. Reprinted with permission.)

The lessons at the agency were taught by Emmeline Snively herself, and she was helped out by Maria Smith and Mrs Gavin Beardsley. Many of the girls attended with their mothers, but as Norma Jeane's was in a mental hospital, this was not a possibility for her. Instead she arrived on her own and on time, eager to begin and anxious to soak up as much knowledge as she possibly could. This enthusiasm impressed Miss Snively and she never forgot it: 'The first day Marilyn attended classes, I knew she would do all right, because she aroused the good nature in people. She would walk in and in her cute, high voice say, "Hello everybody" and everybody would answer "Hello." There was something arresting and sincere about the girl's personality.'

'There was something arresting and sincere about the girl's personality'

Norma Jeane settled into the classes well, and she received lots of extra attention from Miss Snively as a result of seeing her potential and feeling sympathy that she had nobody to help her on her new journey. 'Most of the girls had someone behind them, someone to drive them to different jobs, a father to protect and oversee things,' she said. 'Marilyn had no-one. Only herself. I guess it was because of this that I took a strong interest in the girl. I concentrated on her and she gobbled up every bit of instruction.'

Miss Snively noted that Norma Jeane was wonderful when it came to learning techniques such as make-up, hand positions and body posture, but she had concerns over other aspects of the modelling profession:

> She did have a pleasant personality; what we call an All-American girl kind of personality – cute, wholesome and respectable. There was no sultry sexiness about her. That sex build-up was to come much later, although I did realise immediately that Marilyn would never do as a fashion model. Most fashion models are tall, sophisticated-looking and slim-chested. Marilyn was none of these.

Also a problem was the way the young model walked, which went against everything that a fashion model was ever trained to do.

In the years since her discovery, the reason behind Marilyn's famous 'wiggle walk' has been discussed over and over again, with many theories being put forward, including the possibility that she used to cut part of the heel from one of her shoes, therefore causing her bottom to rock from side to side. Another theory was that the actress had suffered from some kind of mystery illness as a child, resulting in her having a slight limp. This, they say, she emphasised to create a wiggle.

The various theories amused Marilyn, and she herself said there was no mystery surrounding the way she got from A to B, that she had learned to walk as a baby and had been doing it ever since. She did, however, share a fun anecdote about the effect her work had on the boys in her teenage neighbourhood, saying, 'I think I was about twelve when things changed radically. The boys didn't have cars, they had bikes. They'd come by the house and whistle, or they'd honk their little horns. Some had paper routes and I'd always get a free paper.' As for advice on walking like a real woman, Marilyn offered this: 'When you walk, always think UP in front and DOWN in back.'

Miss Snively had her own theory, stating that:

When Marilyn walks her knees lock. She's double-jointed in the knees, so she can't relax and that is why her hips seem to sway when she stalks into a room. She couldn't possibly stand with a relaxed knee like most models, because her knees would lock in a stiff-legged position. Her walk is a result of that locking action every time she takes a step … This she turned into an asset. Many recently published pictures have featured this pose, which for most models would not be acceptable.

Another 'problem' was her smile, which the agency (and several magazine editors) felt made her nose look too long. This was easily rectified, however, as Miss Snively later recalled, 'She smiled too high, that's what was wrong, and it made deep lines around her nose. We taught her how to bring her smile down, and show her lowers.' This resulted in the famous lip quiver that could often be seen in Marilyn's film roles, and which lookalikes and tribute artists often emulate to this day.

1. Norma Jeane outside the factory she worked at before her modelling days. Photographer: David Conover. (From the collection of Kim Goodwin. Permission granted by David Conover Jnr)

Dame And Dane

4. *Norma Jeane with a Great Dane. Photographer: Potter Hueth. (From the collection of Dionne Abraham. Used with permission from Roland Hueth)*

Opposite: 5. Norma Jeane poses in shorts, sweater and skis during location shooting with David Conover. Photographer: David Conover. (From the collection of Kim Goodwin. Used with permission from David Conover Jnr)

6. *Norma Jeane on location with Andre De Dienes. Photographer: Andre De Dienes. (Reproduced with permission of Chuck Murphy: One West Publishing, www.onewestpublishing.com)*

Opposite: 7. Norma Jeane at the pool. Photographer: Richard C. Miller. (Reproduced with permission of Margaret Miller)

8. *Norma Jeane with yellow skirt. Photographer: Richard C. Miller. (Reproduced with the permission of Margaret Miller)*

Finally, there was the continuing problem with her hair, which Miss Snively had already noted. 'It was so curly, so frizzy. It grew so curly it couldn't be managed. When she bent over, nothing happened; not a hair moved.'

While Norma Jeane was eager to soak up any advice that Miss Snively gave her about her smile, she was less happy with what she suggested for her hair: bleach and a permanent straightening solution. Firstly, there was no way the young model could afford the upkeep of such a style, but, secondly, she seemed to have no wish to be made into a glamour girl. 'She was always a believer in naturalness,' wrote Miss Snively, 'and any suggestions about lightening her hair or even styling it met with defeat.'

This page from the 1945–46 Models Bluebook shows Norma Jeane's picture along with her vital statistics. Photographer: David Conover. (From the archive of Ben and Astrid Franse. Permission granted by David Conover Jnr)

TOTTY DAVIS
Age 9—Size 10
4'6"
70 pounds

R. E. Earle
Hair—Light brown
Eyes—Brown

Page Military, Sports, Photography

24

NORMA JEAN DOUGHERTY
12   36
5'6"   24
118   34

David B. Connover
Hair—Blonde
Eyes—Blue

Drama, Photography, Color

25

The agency boss tried desperately to change Norma Jeane's mind, and she was backed up by the other teachers at the school when they explained that her hair was just too curly and would prevent the modelling of hats and other headwear. Still, this was not enough to persuade Norma Jeane to dye it. She made something of a compromise by blow-drying it straighter occasionally, but bleaching and permanently straightening? For now she just wasn't in the least bit interested.

Away from the school there was modelling work to do and fees to pay. In this regard, Miss Snively sent Norma Jeane on her first official assignment as a hostess at an industry show being held at the Pan Pacific Auditorium. Blue Book often supplied models for such events, and Miss Snively later wrote about it in her 1960 catalogue: 'Booth attendants and Queens [are available] for conventions and trade shows … They wear costumes, shorts and sweaters, cocktail dresses and ball gowns as the job requires. Girls are available as demonstrators, couponers and samplers.'

Norma Jeane's job as hostess wasn't particularly glamorous but it did pay, so she dove into it headlong. Described as 'America's annual tribute to the working man', the Industry on Parade exhibition began on Labor Day weekend with a motorcade travelling through downtown Los Angeles, towards Pan Pacific. Various other events were planned throughout the day before the official celebrations began at 8 p.m. and the show declared open for the following ten days.

The idea of the event was to highlight inventions that would be beneficial to 'housewives and businessmen alike' and included many ideas submitted by scientists from all over the United States. One such invention was a Wire Recorder, described as a machine that enabled armed forces to record vital data while under battle conditions. The ideas were interesting and unique, but Norma Jeane was not employed to show off such innovations. Instead she found herself on a stand taken by the Holga Steel Company, talking to visitors, giving out leaflets and showcasing one of the company's items – a steel filing cabinet.

The job may not have been what she wanted to put her energies into in the future, but Norma Jeane was paid $90 for the time she was there, which went a long way towards paying off her modelling course and the agency registration fee. It also promised to be much more fun than working in the munitions factory where she had been employed before her move into modelling, and far less exhausting too.

Described as 'absolutely terrified' by Miss Snively, Norma Jeane travelled to the Pan Pacific Auditorium day after day and looked after the thousands of people who wandered past the booth. Very few photos still exist of the event, but those that do show Norma Jeane wearing two outfits: her sensible, white dress and a longer evening gown, which was probably bought or borrowed especially for the occasion. Photos of her in the white dress must surely have been taken towards the beginning of the job, as she is seen standing shyly next to a table in one and then smiling nervously as she demonstrates the sliding action of the filing-cabinet drawers in the other.

The photograph in the evening dress, however, is a complete turnaround and shows a confident and self-assured young woman, casually standing next to the files and smiling at the camera. 'Marilyn was a wow,' wrote Miss Snively. 'She was kind of a breathless little girl.' When she returned to the agency, Norma Jeane gratefully handed over all her earnings to the agency boss: 'She gave me the whole ninety dollars. Took nothing out for car fare or meals or clothes or anything. "This," she said, "will take care of most of my tuition." I knew at once that Marilyn was a fair and honest and very fine girl, and I decided to get her as much work as I possibly could.'

'I knew at once that Marilyn was a fair and honest and very fine girl, and I decided to get her as much work as I possibly could'

Interestingly, a beauty contest was held during the ten-day event, but while Norma Jeane was more than qualified to win, once again her married status meant that she was unable to enter. This would have surely disappointed her, not only because Miss Snively was always telling girls it would further their careers but also because for the past few years she had been extremely jealous and paranoid about James Dougherty's former girlfriend, Doris Drennen, a beauty queen who had been crowned the 1940 May Queen of Santa Barbara

County. Becoming a contest winner herself would have been a personal triumph, but it was not to be. Marriage was getting in the way of her aspirations, and the resentment continued to build. A year later, another Blue Book model, Jean Brown (who posed with Norma Jeane during several work assignments), was excited to enter the contest herself and was crowned Miss Industry of 1946. The judges included past and future Norma Jeane/Marilyn photographers Earl Moran, Larry Kronquist and Paul Parry.

'Marriage was getting in the way of her aspirations'

In September 1945 (around the same time as she was taking part in the Industry Show) Norma Jeane appeared on camera professionally for the very first time. Shot as a test to evaluate her screen presence, the young model appeared in close-up and full-length shots, wearing a two-piece bathing suit with a bird on the front of the bottom section. Video footage shows her standing in front of palm trees in the grounds of the Ambassador Hotel, turning slightly from side to side and beaming widely. The camera then switches to a closer shot, which shows Norma Jeane wearing a tight red sweater and pearls, again turning from side to side, smiling and lowering her top lip as she had been taught to do in the agency classes.

Other girls tested that day were Phyllis Young, Pat Frazee, Helga Tryggva, Pat Palmer, Alice Sousa, Juanita Beach, Virginia Shelton and Eleanore Everette. All girls appeared on camera for approximately fifteen to twenty seconds, in various places around the exterior of the hotel. They are attractive, but it must be said that out of all of the models featured on the reel it is Norma Jeane who stands out, with a look of determination and hunger that makes it clear she would one day go on to bigger and better things.

After the success of the Industry Show, which prompted the Holga Steel Company to send a glowing report to Miss Snively, Norma Jeane's next job was not as successful and in fact became something of a disaster. The Blue Book girls were known and expected to enter into fashion modelling as much as they could, and Miss Snively wrote about the opportunities in her catalogue:

Learn to have the poise of a model. You study walking, pivots, stairs, hand work, footwork. You learn the difference between whole-sale, retail and fashion show technique. Professional make-up and hairstyling make you into the model you hoped to be. You develop your type through your choice of wardrobe, colour and line. Learn to change your type. Opportunity is given [to] students to partici-pate in fashion shows while you are in training. This not only gives you experience but a business reference as well. Photographs are taken at the shows which students may order at a minimum fee. The studio is set up as a wholesale or designers showroom for your ben-efit. Classes are available for children from four years of age.

For those organisations wishing to put on a fashion show, Miss Snively had everything they needed for a great event: 'Complete show pro-duction – commentator, coordinator, music, models, publicity and photographer are available through the agency,' she wrote. However, none of this proved to be very beneficial to Norma Jeane in the weeks after joining the agency. Miss Snively had previously noted that she was unlikely to ever make a good fashion model on account of her full figure and walking style, but she felt compelled to find out for sure. In that regard she sent the young girl to the beach to take part in a job for the Montgomery Ward catalogue.

Sadly, her initial thoughts about Norma Jeane's lack of skill in that area were proved correct when things did not go to plan, and she was sent back to the agency almost immediately. The young model was confused and upset, especially after her last job had gone so well, but Miss Snively noticed a steely determination underneath the sadness. 'Maybe I'll do better next time,' Norma Jeane told her, which impressed the agency boss. 'Those words really typified her spirit, it was upbeat all the way,' she later wrote. Miss Snively encouraged her to perhaps concentrate on photographic work instead. 'Many times she was turned down on a fashion job because she didn't fit a model size 12. They usually pulled too tight across the front, although they fit perfectly everywhere else. However, she kept trying. Whether she got the job or not she made a friend on every interview.'

One company that did have faith in the young model was Arnolds of Hollywood, which used Norma Jeane to model a rather sombre, conservative suit, on sale at their Hollywood Boulevard store for $16.98. 'Sensationally new!' screamed the advert. 'Smart styling makes it perfect to wear anywhere. 100% wool Shetland fabric gives it that "always fresh" look. Jacket is fully rayon lined. Gored skirt has taped hems and a metal zipper. Four beautiful pastel shades from which to choose. Jackets have contrasting colour inserts in front. Sizes ten to twenty.' The advert was advertised in the likes of *Movieland* magazine and others, and it promised that if the customer was not completely satisfied 'every cent you have paid will be refunded to you immediately'.

Norma Jeane poses in a conservative 'Star Suit' for Arnolds of Hollywood. Unknown photographer. (From the collection of Eric Patry)

Another successful experience came when Norma Jeane was cast to appear in a series of photographs for *Douglas Airview*, a magazine for American Airlines. The photographer for the job was Larry Kronquist, whose speciality was taking colour photos for airline publicity – so he most certainly knew what he was doing. Like several other photographers, Kronquist met Norma Jeane in the gardens of the Ambassador Hotel and was immediately impressed. He approved her for the *Douglas Airview* job and told Miss Snively he liked her so much that he would also like to photograph her 'healthy good looks' in some beach shots with a surfboard. Sadly, the agency boss wrote in her notes that the photographer never did get round to taking them, but he did, however, photograph her for a fashion show later in her modelling career.

The idea of the *Douglas Airview* job was to advertise the plane and show Norma Jeane and other models acting out the role of passengers. Together they were photographed being served by the in-flight assistant and demonstrating how comfortable the flying experience could be. Additionally, there were photos of Norma Jeane applying make-up in the bathroom, while wearing slippers and a robe. Then there were several shots reminiscent of certain scenes in *Some Like It Hot* – a film she made later in her career – showing her sitting on the top bunk of the sleeping quarters. Other photos showed the model reading a magazine with friends and finally being shown to the cloakroom by a flight attendant.

The photographs of the event that were filed away in the Blue Book archive are extremely interesting to see. Not only do they show Norma Jeane in the different poses, but several also provide a behind-the-scenes look at what the shoot was like. On the back of these photographs Miss Snively wrote the names of those involved, which included photographer Larry Kronquist and herself, supervising the models, comparing notes and explaining what they wanted them to do. These photographs demonstrate that not only did Miss Snively take an interest in the careers of her models from within the confines of her office but also found time to go out on jobs with them.

*Douglas Airview magazine employed models to advertise its American Airlines flights.
Here Norma Jeane shows great interest in the stewardess handing milk to a young
mother. Photographer: Larry Kronquist. (From the archive of Ben and Astrid Franse)*

Norma Jeane combs her hair for Douglas Airview, wearing slippers brought to the shoot. Photographer: Larry Kronquist. (From the archive of Ben and Astrid Franse)

Miss Snively kept many negatives in her archives. Sadly, these two show slight damage, but Norma Jeane's beauty shines through regardless. Photographer: Larry Kronquist. (From the archive of Ben and Astrid Franse)

Miss Snively and photographer Larry Kronquist behind the scenes at the Douglas Airview photo shoot. Unknown photographer. (From the archive of Ben and Astrid Franse)

Out in the countryside, Norma Jeane poses against a fence — the epitome of 'the girl next door'. Photographer: Andre De Dienes. (Reproduced with permission of Chuck Murphy: One West Publishing, www.onewestpublishing.com)

While they also show Norma Jeane on her first proper photographic job at the agency, the shots give no sign of the grand scale to which her career would one day climb. What one or two of the photos do show, however, is the suit that Miss Snively had hated so much when she first saw it. But while her heart must have sunk when the model lifted it out of her bag, she would surely have to admit that the shoot – blue suit or not – was a massive success and a big push in the right direction for the fledgling model. Later, the agency boss wrote notes on the back of one of the *Douglas Airview* shots: 'Marilyn's first photo-graphic modelling assignment was with twenty five other models for [an] American Airlines booklet. Fees for this job were applied to her modelling school training.'

After studying the resulting photographs, staff at the Blue Book Agency believed that Norma Jeane would have a good future as a photographic model, as later noted in the archive:

> Miss Snively recognized Marilyn's potentials and promoted her toward this field. While magazine cover work is not the highest paid of the photographic modelling jobs (because much of such work is done on speculation, particularly in the west) it does bring the model quickly into the limelight. If she has any theatrical aspira-tions, magazine cover publicity is her wedge to meet those who can help her on from there.

Marilyn added her own thoughts in 1952, when talking to Liza Wilson: 'I was no longer Norma Jeane, the Human Bean, the skinny target of playmates' jibes. I had filled out some. Too full blown, they said, for high-styled fashion modelling. Bathing suits and men's magazine covers brought in my expenses.'

In November 1945, a young Hungarian pho-tographer by the name of Andre De Dienes arrived in Hollywood. He was an extremely tal-ented man, who enjoyed taking photographs of women in the nude and was eager to do a session of that nature while he was in town. Familiar with Miss Snively's work, Andre telephoned the Blue Book Agency

'I was no longer Norma Jeane, the Human Bean, the skinny target of playmates' jibes'

and asked if she had a model he could photograph over the coming days. Miss Snively immediately thought of Norma Jeane, and while the agency boss did not know if she would ever consent to posing nude, she did know that the model was eager for more work and experience. She was sent over to meet De Dienes at his hotel and the two hit it off immediately. Interestingly, while Andre was used to asking his models to disrobe on a somewhat regular basis, he felt rather shy requesting Norma Jeane to do the same thing. Instead, over the course of several photographic sessions, he took some of the most beautiful girl-next-door shots that the model ever posed for in her entire career.

There is no question that Andre De Dienes had a particular style. One can look at his photos of Marilyn today and know instinctively that they are taken by him. There are shots of her on the beach drawing hearts in the sand, wearing slacks and a sweater. Then she is sitting quietly on a deserted highway, wearing a simple T-shirt and skirt, holding her shoes, with her curly hair in plaits. She is seen wearing the same outfit in a field, leaning against a barbed-wire fence.

As well as black and white shots, the photographer took a variety of colour snaps of Norma Jeane, one of which shows her hair in all its unruly glory, held back with a pretty pink ribbon. But while the colour shots are beautifully vibrant, it was a black and white photograph that provided the model with her first cover picture for a national magazine, as described by Miss Snively in her notes:

> Marilyn Monroe's first magazine cover to be published, when she was known as Norma Jeane Dougherty, was the *Family Circle* – holding a little lamb. Andre De Dienes shot a series of this set-up out in the San Fernando Valley. This followed with a *U.S. Camera* cover shared with actresses Linda Christian and Carol Landis. Marilyn was all covered up in checked slacks and sweater, while the other girls wore the swimsuits. All pics by Andre De Dienes.

In December 1960, *This Week* magazine asked Marilyn to comment on a variety of photographs from their archive. One of the shots was the *Family Circle* picture Miss Snively mentions, and Marilyn shared a rather sad story about the background of the shot:

The lamb I was holding had to die – it was a twin and its mother wouldn't nurse it. It seems a sheep only wants one kid at a time. So I had ambivalent feelings, as you can see. My face looks a little distorted – half smiling, half sad.

In December 1945, much to the disapproval of James Dougherty and his family, the young model embarked on an extended trip with De Dienes, which was lucrative in terms of photos but exhausting, too, and not without incident. 'She was frail mentally and physically,' De Dienes later told the *Los Angeles Times*. 'As soon as she finished her work she would hop back in the car and fall asleep.'

Exhaustion wasn't the only problem they encountered, however. At one point they were chased in the desert by some would-be robbers; they paid a disastrous visit to Norma Jeane's estranged mother, Gladys; they lost a host of photographic equipment; they were pulled over by the police; and, sadly for De Dienes, he fell in love. According to his notes, Norma Jeane fell for him too, and the two slept together during the latter part of the journey. While we cannot confirm the young model's true feelings towards the photographer or the trip itself, we do know that on 15 December she sent a postcard to James Dougherty, calling him Dearest Daddy and expressing how much she missed him. In the card she also showed a desire to one day visit Death Valley – one of the locations of the modelling trip – with her husband, declaring it to be a beautiful place.

Whether or not De Dienes knew about her sending the postcard is unclear, as is the question of whether she sent it to Dougherty out of duty, genuine affection or perhaps even guilt after embarking on the affair. It is true to say that De Dienes fell hard for Norma Jeane over the course of time and even wanted to marry her. Since she was already in an unwanted marriage, however, it is fairly easy to see why she eventually persuaded the photographer that a wedding was not part of her future plans. The model made her feelings clear in a letter she wrote to her friend Jean, almost a year later, in October 1946. In the note Norma Jeane explains that while she likes De Dienes a lot and he does everything he can to help her, she does not wish to get married and, besides, the studio she had just been

signed to wished her to remain single until she had built up a career for herself.

Despite that, the photographer and model forged a very good working relationship, and De Dienes used her on a variety of occasions during the years ahead, including in 1949 when she modelled for him during an East Coast publicity trip. He always thought of his sessions as being the turning point in her career, and he was right. 'I put her face on magazine covers,' he said shortly after her death. 'I made her famous. I loved her … and she never mentioned me – not in fifteen years.'

The fact that the actress did not seem to give him any credit at all in her success as a model tested their working relationship. As a result, De Dienes would write to Marilyn twice in 1960, the second time to berate her sternly for not mentioning him in articles and interviews. She eventually got back in touch, but the relationship was not the same and he never photographed her again. The last time they saw each other was on 1 June 1960, but sadly the meeting ended in cross words and he stormed out of her hotel. The negative outcome of the visit stayed with De Dienes, and he remembered and regretted it for the rest of his life.

'I made her famous. I loved her … and she never mentioned me – not in fifteen years'

Opposite: A playful Norma Jeane at the beach, drawing on the sand. Photographer: Andre De Dienes. (Reproduced with permission of Chuck Murphy: One West Publishing, www. onewestpublishing.com)

FOUR

CROSS MY HEART I DID

Since the beginning of their association, Miss Snively had continually asked Norma Jeane to go from being a brunette to a blonde, but while the agency boss expressed her concerns over and over again, she was still met with resistance. Photographs taken by the Maier Studio around this time show her hair to be still fairly unruly, despite what Miss Snively's feelings were on the matter. Eventually, however, a job came up with photographer Raphael Wolff, which required a model with blonde hair. 'Look darling,' Miss Snively told Norma Jeane, 'if you really intend to go places in this business, you've just got to bleach and straighten your hair because now your face is a little too round and a hair job will lengthen it. Don't worry about money, I'll keep you working.'

Wolff hired Norma Jeane for a shampoo advertisement on the understanding that she would sort out her hair once and for all. When he offered to pay for the process too, Norma Jeane finally relented and agreed to go to the Frank and Joseph salon in Hollywood to begin the process. Contrary to popular belief, Norma Jeane did not go from brunette to golden blonde overnight. Instead it took a process of several treatments, each one designed to make her hair go lighter and straighter over a period of time.

Norma Jeane sitting on her bottom with legs out, wearing bikini. Photographer: H Maier Studio. (From the collection of Kim Goodwin)

In February 1946, the first part of the process was applied and included a straight permanent to make the hair more manageable, along with a regular permanent on the ends. Frank and Joseph were thrilled with the results, and Norma Jeane posed for several shampoo adverts for them. Meanwhile, Miss Snively loved the way it made her client look: 'It was bleached to take it out of the obscurity of dishwater blonde,' she wrote. 'From this treatment Marilyn emerged a truly golden girl … From this point she went into her bathing suit stage, and the demand for her was simply terrific. She averaged, I should say, $150 a week, and men began talking to her about going into the motion picture game.'

One of the first people to snap Norma Jeane after the first part of her transformation was Bill Burnside, a young man from Scotland who was in Hollywood on business. He just happened to meet the model when she was at the Bernard of Hollywood studio, where she was posing in a series of glamour shots. The two got along well together, and Burnside asked if she would like to be photographed by his friend in advertising, Paul Hesse. She said yes and travelled out to Malibu to pose for him.

Sadly, Hesse took one look at Norma Jeane and absurdly declared her 'too fat'. This bizarre comment quite rightly made her upset, so Burnside took her to the beach and photographed her with his own equipment. 'She always loved the camera,' he later said. 'It soothed her.' Burnside would take Norma Jeane's photograph again during another of his trips to Hollywood, this time in 1948, and later claimed to have had an on-off affair with her. At the end of their friendship she is said to have written him a poem entitled 'I could have loved you once'.

Another photographer who snapped Norma Jeane around this time was Erwin Steinmeyer, who ran the Steinie Photography studio at the Ambassador

Norma Jeane with the staff of Frank and Joseph, where she had her hair bleached for the first time. Photographer: H Maier Studio. (From the collection of Maria Musikka)

Hotel. 'Photography in better taste' was his motto, but apart from that Erwin Steinmeyer remains an elusive figure, and he does not seem to have made headlines or had any kind of media attention at all. In fact, so lacking is his presence that to this day there are discussions as to whether or not his name was Edwin or Erwin, though historical records confirm it to be the latter. The 1940's census tells us that he was born in Kansas and, shortly before opening his studio, was working as a commercial artist in Los Angeles, sharing an apartment with his lodger, Jack Angel.

Aside from that, Mr Steinmeyer is something of a mystery; nevertheless, the photographs he took of Norma Jeane are still interesting because at times they almost take on the look of candid family snapshots. Wearing a plain-white dress, and then shorts and a bikini top, he snapped her in the grounds of the Ambassador Hotel, looking

Norma Jeane in a seductive pose, wearing gloves. Photographer: Edwin 'Steinie' Steinmeyer. (From the collection of Dionne Abraham)

Opposite: A radiant Norma Jeane. Photographer: Edwin 'Steinie' Steinmeyer. (From the collection of Kim Goodwin)

happy and relaxed in her surroundings. More formal shots were taken in his studio; during the shoot Norma Jeane posed in a variety of actor-inspired headshots, some of the first ever taken of her in that style.

As we have already established, Miss Snively was a very astute and all-seeing businesswoman who knew when an opportunity was staring her in the face. With Norma Jeane's new, lighter hair, she saw that the model's career could be 'launched' once again – she actually told several photographers that Norma Jeane had just started out and was looking for her first big break. This was not entirely true, of course, but the new blonde hair made it possible for this white lie to take credence. Miss Snively wrote about this period, later in her career:

> I had many friends among the photographers and illustrators. They are always interested in discovering new models. Naturally both Marilyn and I were interested in her being discovered so I would call and describe her and tell them she was brand new. She was changing so rapidly that she was new all the time.

This quote is particularly true when it comes to her dealings with Joseph Jasgur, a very talented and respected man who had a studio in Hollywood. He was well versed in the art of taking celebrity shots and was known as the 'Demon photographer' because of his knack of getting a photograph out of the most camera-shy of people. He was easy to talk to and an expert at making sure his subjects remained relaxed

during the sessions. In 1992 he told the Marilyn Lives Society fan club about how his first meeting with the young model came to be:

In March 1946, my close friend Emmeline Snively of the Blue Book Model School, phoned and asked a favour of me. She told me about the poor young girl who visited her, who wanted to be a model. She had no photos, no money to pay for any, etc. and she didn't know anything about this young girl. I asked a few questions, and then told Ms Snively to send her over and I would shoot some tests at no charge. [I would] give this girl some free prints, and some for herself and also give her a detailed report on Norma Jeane, as to how she photographed: cooperative; how she acted in front of the camera; tense, etc. etc. In simple words, I would evaluate her and tell Ms Snively whether I thought I could do some good photos of her and create a good portfolio to help her out (at no cost to either). Ms Snively liked my idea and sent Norma Jeane over to see me.

When Norma Jeane arrived at his studio, it was getting towards the end of the working day, and at first she was nervous, but became calmer after speaking for a few moments with Jasgur. He was not particularly impressed with the young model and later told Miss Snively that she was too thin to be a glamour girl. However, he kept his feelings to himself in front of Norma Jeane and instead asked if she would like to pose for him in the alley behind his studio, just off North Poinsettia Place. She agreed and he took some beautiful close-ups of her, wearing a pale sweater and a beret. An interesting point about this session is that the building where Norma Jeane posed is still in existence today, and almost seventy years later, fans continue to make the pilgrimage to see the spot and have their own photographs taken there too.

'I made four test exposures,' Jasgur said, 'and took the hungry girl out for some food, while my wet negatives were drying. We spoke for quite a while at the restaurant, and then I brought her into my lab where she watched me print the first test photos of her. Norma Jeane was quite impressed with the final prints I gave to her and to Ms Snively. She was so happy, she hugged and kissed me on the cheek.'

Opposite: Norma Jeane close-up. Photographer: Edwin 'Steinie' Steinmeyer. (Top: from the collection of Kim Goodwin; Bottom: from the archive of Ben and Astrid Franse)

Several other sessions were planned with Jasgur, among them a trip to the beach and some fun shots at the top of Don Lee Towers above the Hollywood sign. 'I told Norma Jeane I could get her to the top of Hollywood,' he said in 1992. 'This really impressed her. I did do it four days later. I took her to the roof top of a radio station on top of the Hollywood Hills.' The comical shots taken at Don Lee were done, he told Miss Snively, because he still believed Norma Jeane was too thin to ever be a fully fledged pin-up. In fact, so concerned was Jasgur that he sent her out for hamburgers in an effort to get her to eat more.

After the sessions, the photographer reported back to the agency boss and told her that he felt the young model's smile needed some work and her hair should be lightened further. 'I told Ms Snively I felt that Norma Jeane should definitely become a blonde,' Jasgur said. 'We discussed this for a couple of hours, and the end result – Norma Jeane became the blonde.' These changes were evident in another session Jasgur did with the young model, this time in a job especially for the Blue Book Model Agency.

Miss Snively continued to enjoy using the life ring with the words 'Blue Book Models Hollywood' emblazoned on the side to publicise her business. So it was that in 1946 she invited Joe Jasgur to take some shots of her models in the grounds of the hotel, with Norma Jeane as the main feature. Posing alongside several other models, the much-lighter-haired girl was photographed in many positions, including sitting with her back to the life ring and holding it around her waist. Because the photos were taken as a Blue Book publicity gimmick, Jasgur gave Miss Snively a copy of the negatives. Once Norma Jeane became famous, he also signed a release form:

Consent and Release: In consideration for value received I hereby authorize Emmeline Snively to use, publish, sell or otherwise dispose of any pictures taken by me of Norma Jean [sic] Dougherty, also known as Marilyn Monroe, without further compensation. Signed: Joseph Jasgur. Date: Dec 10, 53.

Norma Jeane posing in the gardens of the Ambassador Hotel holding the Blue Book Models life ring. Photographer: Joseph Jasgur. (From the archive of Ben and Astrid Franse, reproduced with permission from the Joseph Jasgur Estate)

Norma Jeane and fellow Blue Book model in swimsuit and heels, holding the Blue Book Models life ring. Photographer: Joseph Jasgur. (From the archive of Ben and Astrid Franse, reproduced with permission from the Joseph Jasgur Estate)

Norma Jeane with model Jean Brown and life ring. Photographer. Joseph Jasgur. (From the archive of Ben and Astrid Franse, reproduced with permission from the Joseph Jasgur Estate)

A smiling Norma Jeane holding the Blue Book Models life ring. Photographer: Joseph Jasgur. (From the archive of Ben and Astrid Franse, reproduced with permission from the Joseph Jasgur Estate)

Norma Jeane and another Blue Book model sitting symmetrically either side of the life ring. Photographer: Joseph Jasgur. (From the archive of Ben and Astrid Franse, reproduced with permission from the Joseph Jasgur Estate)

1:-AMBASSADOR HOTEL, LOS ANGELES, CALIFORNIA

The graduation photos were taken in gardens at the Ambassador Hotel, such as the ones shown in this postcard. (From the archive of Ben and Astrid Franse)

The reverse side of one of the lost photos from the Joseph Jasgur collection. This shows that the images were taken at graduation. (From the archive of Ben and Astrid Franse, reproduced with permission from the Joseph Jasgur Estate)

In his 1991 book, *The Birth of Marilyn*, Jasgur describes how he once loaned several photographs to Norma Jeane, but she did not return them to him. He does not describe what they looked like, but in the book he prophesises that they may be found in a long-lost cardboard box, sometime in the future. 'Somebody's in for a big surprise some day,' he wrote.

'My heart almost stood still when I read that comment,' says co-author and archive-keeper Astrid Franse.

Jasgur photo release for Miss Snively. (From the archive of Ben and Astrid Franse, reproduced with permission from the Joseph Jasgur Estate)

The reason for her shock is understandable when we hear what she found in the Blue Book files. There were seven photographs that were given to Miss Snively after the life ring session, some of which were later published in Jasgur's book and have become a part of his life and legend. Others, however, do not appear in his portfolio and could very well be the ones he is referring to in *The Birth of Marilyn*. The changes in style and pose of each picture are subtle but nevertheless unique. 'I truly believe these are the lost photographs, as they came with six transparencies too,' Astrid says. 'I believe that we didn't find the box, but the box found Ben and me.'

Coming close on the heels of the early Joseph Jasgur photos was an extraordinarily beautiful series with photographer Richard Miller. Miller had come to camera work after moving on from a career in acting. As with Jasgur, it had been Miss Snively who put him in touch with Norma Jeane, telling the man that she was very cute and he just had to meet her. When he did, Miller agreed with the agency boss's assessment, and he took Norma Jeane on several photography expeditions during the coming months.

The photos taken by Miller are all very different in style and background. While some photographers preferred to shoot Norma Jeane in similar, familiar settings, Miller was very keen to take her

Opposite: Photographer Joseph Jasgur, as he looked around the time Norma Jeane knew him. (From the collection of the Joseph Jasgur Estate, reproduced with permission from the Joseph Jasgur Estate)

photograph with as many different looks and in as many locations as he possibly could. The result was a variety of shots at the beach, a pool, in a studio, beside a fire, on a rock and everywhere in-between. For the sessions the young model wore a variety of outfits, including bikinis, sweaters, checked shirts (complete with hat and binoculars), blouses, skirts and a whole lot more. One photograph was supposed to show her wearing a bikini with a short skirt, but Norma Jeane opted not to include the skirt with the outfit. The result was dynamite, and many young men began to storm the beach where she was posing; Miller and his model had to make a quick getaway.

As a result of the varied settings and looks, Richard Miller was able to show the many different sides of Norma Jeane, transforming her from the girl-next-door she once was to the glamorous starlet she was quickly turning into. Interestingly, several of the photos taken during the sessions show the young model wearing the same wedding dress she had worn whilst tying the knot with James Dougherty. This rather unusual look was later sold as a cover for *Personal Romances* magazine, and it was probably the last time she ever wore the dress. Another unusual shot shows Norma Jeane in a ruffled top with a choker pendant around her neck. Two of these later photographs have become famous and show the model looking towards the camera, one boasting a big, open-mouthed smile, while the other shows her mouth closed in a small grin.

'transforming her from the girl-next-door she once was to the glamorous starlet she was quickly turning into'

Opposite: Miss Snively kept the negative for this Richard C. Miller photo in her archive for the rest of her life. Norma Jeane's beauty shines through. (From the archive of Ben and Astrid Franse, reproduced with permission from Margaret Miller)

Both photos are in colour with a flowery print background, but another version – this time black and white – was also taken that day, and the negative and print were presented to Miss Snively by Richard Miller. This photo shows Norma Jeane turned slightly away from the camera, but with the same smile as before. On the back of the shot, Miss Snively wrote, 'Marilyn Monroe, December 1945 – January 1946. She looked like this. Hair was still pretty unmanageable, face a little too round – very wholesome though.' It should be noted that Miss Snively got the date wrong; the photograph was actually taken between March and April 1946, but this was just a slight oversight on her part.

Marilyn Monroe 500
1945 –
Dec. 1945
③ January –1946 –

she looked like this–

Hair was still
pretty unmanageable,
face a little too
round – very
wholesome, though

'she was always unwilling
to pose in the nude'

Richard Miller loved working with Norma Jeane and told the agency boss that he liked her better than any girl he had ever photographed. He entered one of his photos into a competition in *Cosmopolitan*, entitled 'My Favourite Picture', but while he thought it should win, the editors believed differently. They told the photographer that his model just wasn't cute enough, but that did not alter his opinion of her one iota.

While Norma Jeane was becoming well known to various photographers around Hollywood and beyond, she was always unwilling to pose in the nude. Swimsuits were fine; bikinis were great, but no outfit at all? She was apparently appalled at the thought. However, by the time the model met Earl Moran in spring 1946 this all changed.

Moran was a well-respected, if not slightly controversial, artist and photographer. Born in Iowa, he studied his craft in Chicago and New York, before signing to calendar company Brown and Bigelow in the early 1930s. His artwork for them involved pin-up models in a combination of fun and cheeky pictures, along the lines of fellow artist Gil Elvgren. His way of working was impressive: he would first photograph his models in a variety of different poses, then he would use these pictures to build up a portrait of what he wanted to convey on the calendar. Sometimes the art very much resembled the photo, while at other times it was merely inspired by the original piece. But regardless of how the portraits were put together, Moran's work was extremely well done, and his pictures – both original and prints – are very much in demand with collectors today.

When Norma Jeane walked into his Los Angeles studio in spring 1946, he didn't think much of her. 'She was not particularly pretty,' he later said. However, this soon changed when he saw the girl in front of his camera and realised just how much she loved to pose. 'For her it was acting,' Earl said. 'She was better than anyone else. Emotionally she did everything right; she expressed just what I wanted.'

Some of the photos taken of Norma Jeane during her time with Moran show her in fairly regular poses, such as reclining on a chair, winking or wearing a bathing suit. However, some are very different to others taken either at that time or beyond and show the actress in a variety of irregular positions. For instance, there is a photograph of her kneeling in a fruit basket, while another shows her wearing a bolero and holding a mask. Others have Norma Jeane putting on a shoe or attired in a nightshirt while carrying a candle; then she is seen pretending to dive from a board, with the use of sofa cushions and a swimming cap as props. In every one of the photos, there is absolutely no doubt that she was having copious amounts of fun. Earl's observation that the model loved to pose is apparent in every shot he took. She looks happy, playful and full of hope for the future.

'She looks happy, playful and full of hope for the future'

While Moran often liked Norma Jeane to pose wearing bathing costumes or other scant outfits, he also asked her to pose nude. While she would later say that all requests for such work were turned down, this is actually not true. The model certainly did pose nude for Earl Moran, though perhaps she did not count these as official photograph sessions, as they were eventually turned into artwork rather than released as photographic nudes. Miss Snively remembered:

Previous spread: The small towel Marilyn is holding barely covers her chest as she leans forward in a chair. Photographer: Earl Moran. A glamorous nude shot of Marilyn kneeling in a fruit basket – a far cry from the wholesome images of her earlier days as a model. Photographer: Earl Moran. (Both are from the the archive of Ben and Astrid Franse)

While Norma Jeane was appearing on many magazines she still needed additional work and Miss Snively sent her to artist Earl Moran. Earl drew calendar pictures at this time and Norma Jeane worked for him both as a life model and posed for photographs to choose the pose best suited to the month he was illustrating. Models received $5.00 an hour for posing, which was the going rate at the time. Earl kept shoes and dresses to be used for modelling and once gave Norma Jeane a pair of shoes because the ones she was in were coming apart. In addition to the calendars which were done in pastel chalks, Mr Moran did oil paintings of nudes. Marilyn posed for several of the paintings long before the infamous nude calendar pose for photographer Tom Kelley.

Some of the Moran nude photos show Marilyn covering her chest with her arm, while others show her bare breasts very much on display as she bends backwards over a bench. All of the shots are tasteful; sometimes they are cheeky and often quite saucy, but perhaps the most beautiful is one taken for a portrait entitled 'Lady in the Light'. The light and shadows used on the photo, which was taken to accompany the portrait, makes it hard to have a clear view of the model, but it does appear to show a young Marilyn Monroe in profile, looking up towards the ceiling, with one arm bent up towards her head. She is totally nude, but with the help of the lighting, the photograph keeps her dignity intact. It is interesting to note, however, that when Moran worked on the painting afterwards he gave Marilyn a few more curves than she had in real life and more voluptuous breasts.

During the course of her acting career, Marilyn was to talk about her nude modelling days rather a lot, though it always seemed to focus around the one session she admitted to – a 1949 calendar shot with photographer Tom Kelley. However, much of what she revealed about her feelings towards posing nude seems to have been about the earlier Moran sessions too. She would later tell several reporters, including Ben Hecht, that being naked in front of the camera released any depression or sadness she may be feeling at the time. 'I was glad I hadn't eaten much in the past few days because the pictures would show a real washboard stomach,' she said.

Opposite: Marilyn poses for artist Earl Moran, who is seen with an ever-present pipe in his mouth. Photographer: Joseph Jasgur. (From the collection of Michelle Morgan). Reproduced with permission from the Joseph Jasgur Estate.

The relationship between Earl Moran and Marilyn was a good one, and it always remained professional. However, at the time they were working together, the photographer was embroiled in a bitter divorce from his wife, Mura Moran, over an incident with a model in 1944. The story went that Mrs Moran arrived at his New York studio unexpectedly one day to find model Chili Williams running around in the nude, while Earl was only wearing shorts. According to his wife, there was no camera in sight and she was left without any doubt as to what was going on. The scandalous tale was denied by the model herself, who branded the charge as 'Ridiculous. I, like hundreds of other models in New York, worked for Earl Moran but I never so much as went out with him.' Furthermore, Williams said that she had only ever seen Mrs Moran once and she most definitely had her clothes on during that occasion. 'I was not [nude] and I have never worked for any artist or photographer without attire,' she said.

All this had happened several years before Norma Jeane walked into Moran's Los Angeles studio, but the custody and alimony issues related to the separation were still very much going on when she was working with him. Eventually, it all went to court and the judge declared that there was 'no evidence of immorality on the part of Miss Williams'. The court then heard another woman – Bernice Page – describe how she had met Mrs Moran and found her to be 'constantly angry', and once told her, 'so you're the one who kept Earl out. Well you can have him.' The incident happened, Page said, after accompanying Moran to a have an innocent drink with some friends. Furthermore, it was also disclosed that Mrs Moran herself had been seen out in the company of someone who was not her husband. The case with his estranged wife was eventually settled, much to Moran's relief, and he moved on with his career. This of course included photographing and painting Norma Jeane on a fairly regular basis.

Many other cameramen had a chance to photograph Norma Jeane during this time, including Laszlo Willinger, who was a very popular photographer and a big hit with his models. Annabelle Stanford worked with him many times during her own modelling career and described him as 'a wonderful, charming, decent and delightful man'. Miss Snively later wrote about him in her notes: 'Laszlo Willinger's playsuit photo appeared on a *Laff* magazine cover, with the Pacific Ocean as the background. Willinger thought Marilyn was "just what the doctor ordered" in a model and he sold many covers both before and after her first contract with Twentieth Century Fox.' It would seem that the feeling was mutual, as Norma Jeane specifically asked Miss Snively if he had been in touch during a letter she wrote to her several months later.

Willinger took some interesting photos of the young model, many of which were swimsuit, pin-up-style shots. Others, however, were more like Earl Moran's in style; they were fairly risqué and showed her topless, though discreetly covering her breasts with her arms, hats or, at one point, a Hawaiian garland. He even took studio publicity head-shots a few years later, some of which are the most beautiful publicity shots ever taken of Marilyn Monroe. Some years later, in a documentary entitled *Marilyn: Beyond The Legend*, the photographer described meeting Norma Jeane: 'It was in 1946, Miss Snively had a little agency and she called and said "I have a girl and I think she might be interesting" so I said send her over.' When Norma Jeane walked into his studio, Laszlo did not think a great deal of her, describing her as nice but nothing great. However, he did some tests and liked the results. 'From that time on I used her for years,' he said. 'She had one bad front tooth which I had fixed at my expense, and her hair was kinky which someone else fixed, but she was a very good model.' Laszlo guessed that he must have had her on about a hundred magazine covers, though this could have been an exaggeration. Still, he was right in saying that long before she became Marilyn Monroe, Norma Jeane had already built up quite a following, based on her face and figure alone.

Bruno Bernard (aka Bernard of Hollywood) was another photographer who worked with Norma Jeane before, during and after this time. He was a splendid photographer: a legendary man who snapped many stars over the years, including Clark Gable, Jane Russell and Elvis Presley. His photographs of Norma Jeane run the gamut from

'long before she became Marilyn Monroe, Norma Jeane had already built up quite a following, based on her face and figure alone'

swimsuit sessions through to glamorous poses at a charity event, and even some of the famous skirt-blowing scene in 1954. Miss Snively wrote a few lines about Bernard's work with Marilyn in her notes: 'He enjoyed working with her. She was easy to pose and had lots of sparkle. Bernard used her for many magazine covers, both indoors and out.'

Norma Jeane put a lot of time and effort into learning her craft, as Mrs Snively later wrote in the archive: 'Marilyn took direction well. Let's have a big smile – open eyes – moist lips. Her expressions improved. She studied her photographs, criticised positions and expression. She took modelling seriously, as she does her acting now.'

While she was beginning to make something of a splash with some of her photos, Norma Jeane did not make that many magazine covers at first. 'It may seem contradictory,' Miss Snively said, 'but her pictures were hard to sell. New York picture agents weren't too sold on her. Magazine art directors pointed out her bad angles. Nevertheless the photographers themselves, from rank amateur to famous professionals, were confident of her natural appeal. They were sold on her vibrant personality, colouring, and on her clean scrubbed "American Girl" looks. They recognised that she had that certain something that registers on film.'

In 1953 Marilyn surprisingly told reporter Logan Gourlay that she was never too successful as a model. History, however, proves otherwise. Because of the dedication to her craft, coupled with the photographers' belief in her, Norma Jeane eventually began to appear in and on a whole host of magazines. 'Many cover shots came out featuring Marilyn about the same time,' Miss Snively wrote. 'But they all looked decidedly different. If you didn't know her you wouldn't have recognized some of them, although they were posed within an eighteen month period.'

Marilyn later remembered that most of the photos used of her were for 'men's magazines. Magazines with cover girls who are not flat-chested. I was on *See* four or five months in a row. Each time they changed my name. One month I was Norma Jeane Dougherty; the second month I was Jean Norman. I don't know what all [the] names they used [were] but I must have looked different each time. There were different poses – outdoors, indoors, but mostly just sitting, looking over the Pacific. You looked at those pictures and you didn't see much ocean, but you saw a lot of me.'

Over the next decade, Norma Jeane's photograph would appear on magazines all over the world, long after she had changed her name to Marilyn Monroe and achieved major stardom. Back in the mid to late 1940s, her international covers included the likes of *Leader Magazine* in England, *Pour Tous Films* in France, *de Prins reporter* in Holland, *Intimita* in Italy and *Hela Varlden* in Sweden. Once she had enough covers under her belt, Miss Snively thought it would be good publicity for Norma Jeane and the agency if she wrote a press release about her achievement. A copy, complete with hand-written corrections and amendments, was filed in the archive:

'You looked at those pictures and you didn't see much ocean, but you saw a lot of me'

FOR IMMEDIATE RELEASE

Blue Book Model: Norma Jeane Dougherty proves to be California Model Extraordinary, by appearing on five National Magazine Covers in one month. Norma Jeane is a healthy product of the San Fernando Valley.

VITAL STATISTICS: Height – 5'6", Weight – 120 lbs, Bust – 36, Waist 24, Hips 34. WHOO! WHOO!

Light hair and blue eyes and a beautiful smile. What more could you want? She is currently gracing the covers of: THE FAMILY CIRCLE, LAFF, U.S. CAMERA with CAROL LANDIS, PAGEANT, SALUTE.

WE SALUTE YOU NORMA JEANE!

To go with the celebration of being one of the most successful Blue Book models of all time, Miss Snively arranged for photographer Bill Harvey to visit the Ambassador to take snaps of Norma Jeane surrounded by some of her featured magazines. The model sat in the grounds of the hotel wearing a favourite white bikini and holding a card with the words 'Blue Book Models Hollywood' printed on it. Miss Snively then placed a series of magazine covers around the very proud model.

Miss Snively was exceptionally proud of her models. Here, she is seen next to her new car with a board full of her clients' work. Unknown photographer. (From the archive of Ben and Astrid Franse)

Opposite: Norma Jeane poses happily with her early magazine covers. In one photo she accidentally blinked; a problem Miss Snively rectified with the help of scissors and glue. Photographer: Bill Harvey. (From the archive of Ben and Astrid Franse)

At least three photographs were taken by Bill Harvey that day – one standing and the others sitting. When developed, however, there was a rather large problem, as the best-seated picture showed Norma Jeane with her eyes firmly closed. Miss Snively had two options: she could use the second-best photograph or chose a more inventive way to rectify the problem. In the end, the more creative solution won. Taking a pair of scissors, the agency boss cut out the head of the second photo, and pasted it on top of the one with closed eyes. Now the better photograph had a beautiful face with open eyes and was ready to be published in magazines around the country.

Miss Snively kept the secret of this photograph hidden from the public for the rest of her life, and it was only discovered when co-author Astrid Franse found it in the archive many years later. The smiling photograph was framed, and it wasn't until Astrid travelled to a television studio that the truth was revealed. When she arrived for the interview, she was shocked to discover that the fake head had fallen off the photograph and was now residing at the bottom of

the frame. A secret of Marilyn's modelling career had been revealed, along with an example of the tricks photographers and agency bosses came up with, years before the Photoshop era.

Over the next year or so Norma Jeane found her niche in being a cover girl rather than a fashion model. However, during her career she was also used extensively for print advertisements, both as Norma Jeane and as Marilyn. During her modelling years, her photograph appeared on adverts for many different products and stores, such as the aforementioned Arnolds of Hollywood, as well as the following:

* Argoflex cameras. These print adverts included a photograph of Norma Jeane taken by Andre De Dienes. The model could be seen kneeling next to a tree, wearing a pale sweater and checked trousers, smiling at the camera, while underneath the advert explained that the Argoflex 'shows you the picture before you take it'.

* AlbumColor Prints. This tri-color laboratory, situated on North Vermont Avenue in Hollywood, used a Richard Miller snap of Norma Jeane to advertise their photo reproduction in 1946. 'Your memories will live in color with AlbumColor Prints,' it said.

* Pepsodent toothpaste. Another De Dienes print, this time showing a close-up of Norma Jeane, was used to show the 'sparkling white teeth' that could be obtained by using Pepsodent. 'My teeth really are whiter!' the model appeared to say.

* Emde Aluminium Protectochrome Mounts. This modelling job saw Norma Jeane wearing a sweater while showing off an album of photographic mounts. The advert came in two forms: one was printed in various magazines, and the other was used as a fold-out pamphlet, designed to sit on a shop counter or be given out to photography students. 'Try Emde Mounts for a new thrill in mounting pleasure,' the advert said. 'A picture worth taking is worth protecting.'

* Tru-Glo Liquid Make-up. A modelling photograph showing Norma Jeane in a yellow bathing suit was later used in an advertisement for Tru-Glo, calling it 'Marilyn Monroe's Glamour Secret!'.

* Nesbitt's Orange. What appears to be an Earl Moran portrait of a blonde Norma Jeane was used to advertise the orange drink

in 1946. Seen smiling while holding a bottle up towards her face, the picture was used as an advertising calendar for the product.

* Crème Nivea. The famous moisturiser, still used around the world today, was advertised by Norma Jeane in approximately 1946. The young woman was photographed on a boat with other models, including Annabelle Stanford, during the full-colour campaign.

* Jantzen Swimwear. Marilyn was photographed enjoying a day at the beach with another model, pretending to fish and holding up her catch. The results were used to advertise the Jantzen Swimwear range in 1947.

* Dolly Madison Wine. In 1947 Marilyn posed for artist Gordon Provonsha, who painted her as a western-style barmaid to publicise Dolly Madison Wine. She was photographed also holding several bottles on a tray, with her blonde hair tied back from her face.

* National Postmasters Convention. From 12–16 October 1947 the Postmasters Convention took place, and Marilyn was involved in publicity for the event. The adverts consisted of an 'Official Souvenir Post Card' showing Marilyn, starlet Donna Hamilton and host Mike Fanning all standing next to a TWA plane. Between the two models was a photograph of a man's body with a cut-out head and the words 'Me' inserted onto it. The handwritten wording read, 'Oh Boy, what a wonderful way to be greeted.'

* B-1 Lemon-Lime Soda. A portrait, fairly similar in style to ones photographer Paul Parry used to advertise Mission Orange Drink, appeared for B-1 Lemon-Lime Soda. The photograph showed Norma Jeane putting the bottle up towards her mouth while a young man, in overcoat and hat, smiles on.

* So-Rite Fashion Catalogue. Despite never taking to full-time fashion modelling, the young woman was used to advertise suits and overcoats for So-Rite whilst publicising the film *Love Happy* in 1949. The fashion spread featured in the fall catalogue for the company and gave Marilyn a colour cover photo, wearing a leopard-print coat with fur trim. The suits also appeared in *Photoplay* magazine, with the title: 'On the fashion goal-line: A suit and coat that will score on any occasion.'

Marilyn models a calf-length coat in Photoplay magazine. Unknown photographer. (From the collection of Marco van der Munnik)

Marilyn looks like a young businesswoman in this striped jacket and skirt, also in Photoplay. Unknown photographer. (From the collection of Marco van der Munnik)

✳ Kyron. Also during 1949, Love Happy publicity, a large print advert, appeared in newspapers to advertise Kyron slimming pills. A bikini-clad Marilyn was used to bolster claims of what customers could look like if they chose to lose weight the Kyron way.

While her modelling career was rising to unprecedented heights, Norma Jeane did not seem to have any ambitions to take her career further. 'She had no interest in making movies,' wrote Miss Snively and her secretary Joyce Ryan. 'She thought of herself as a model.' This reluctance to go into acting was most certainly a new thing, as Marilyn later said many times that she had wanted to act since she was a very small girl. 'I always wanted to be an actress,' she said in 1960. 'When I was just nine or ten, living with foster parents, I used to shut myself in my little room and act out scenes from the movies I'd seen. I didn't have any conviction that I'd be a big star, I just wanted to be an actress and hoped. Kept on hoping.'

'I just wanted to be an actress and hoped. Kept on hoping'

The fact that Norma Jeane took to telling Miss Snively that she had no ambitions of being an actress is intriguing, but it could be because of an incident that happened around this time, which she later wrote about in 1953. Apparently Norma Jeane was walking down the street one day when a man pulled his Cadillac up next to her. He rolled down the window and told the young woman that she was so beautiful she should be in the movies. 'That was the first time I'd ever heard it,' she said, 'so it didn't sound corny to me.'

The man added that he worked for the Goldwyn Studio and she should come over for an audition. Norma Jeane told him to contact Miss Snively at Blue Book if he wanted to take the matter further, and then went about her day.

'I was modelling at that time,' she said. 'And I asked the people who ran the agency where I got my jobs, what they thought of his offer. The manager called the studio but never was able to get in touch with my would-be benefactor. However, the wolf called the agency and I made an appointment to go to his office on Saturday afternoon.'

Unfortunately, his studio space turned out to be a rented suite and the role he had for her was non-existent. Instead, the 'executive' persuaded her to pose in a variety of inappropriate positions, while reading a script. 'All the poses had to be reclining, although the words I was reading didn't seem to call for that position. Even as naïve as I was then, I soon figured out that this wasn't the way to get a job in the movies. He was getting sillier by the minute and I manoeuvred over toward the door and made a hasty exit.'

Another exit was being planned by spring 1946, when Norma Jeane's marriage to James Dougherty was all but over. He had returned from the service permanently and everything was changing,

> Marilyn took direction well. Lets have a big smile -- open eyes ---- moist lips. Her expressions improved . She studied her photographs, criticized positions, and expression. She took modeling seriously., as she does her acting now.

> MAGAZINE COVER GIRL
>
> Marilyn Monroe's first magazine cover to be published , when she was known as Norma Jean Dougherty,)was the Family Circle.- holding a little lamb. Andre de Dienes shot a series of this set-up out in the San Fernando Valley.
>
> May 1946
> This followed with a U. S. Camera cover shared with actresses Linda Christian and Carol Landis. Marilyn was all covered up in checked slacks and sweater, while the other girls wore the swim suits. All pig's by Andre de Dienes.
>
> Next Lazlo Willinger's play suit photo appeared on Laff Magazine cover, with the Pacific Ocean as the Background. Willinger thought Marilyn was "just what the doctor ordered" in a model, and he sold many covers both before and after her first contract with 20th Century Fox .
>
> How she felt about covers

Two pages of the many notes Miss Snively kept about her star pupil. (From the archive of Ben and Astrid Franse)

though not often for the best as far as the young model was concerned. Miss Snively wrote about this episode in her notes:

> The legend of Marilyn Monroe alleges that Norma Jeane's marriage at sixteen was to get away from the series of foster homes she had been shuttled from. While this was probably true, I could tell that it was a deep love for James Dougherty that caused the floods of tears to burst for Norma Jeane. Jim's return from service was a wonderful time in her life and for a short time the happiest period, but it was short lived. Jim insisted that Norma Jeane quit modelling. I talked with Norma Jeane for hours and told her that she must make her own decisions. I pointed out that a model's career lasted for only a few years and that a wife and mother had a lifetime contract. However, Norma Jeane chose the role of the model. It offered her something she had never known before.

Another development occurred when Norma Jeane told her mentor that perhaps she did want to be an actress after all. This is something that is detailed in the archive:

> Miss Snively felt that as she was becoming quite well known she needed a manager to further her career. Norma Jeane was still somewhat naïve in so far as the law of the jungle called Hollywood. Miss Snively took her to meet her friend, Helen Ainsworth. Miss Ainsworth was associated with a group of corporate agents. She looked at Marilyn some and was impressed by the quality she had to photograph in colour.

Helen Ainsworth was a legend in her own right. Over the years she had dabbled in acting and then took on a career as a hat maker during the 1930s. It was during this time that she unintentionally became embroiled in the investigation into actress Thelma Todd's death, due to the fact that Todd had visited Ainsworth's hat shop just days before she passed away. That depressing case behind her, the hat maker eventually found her way into work as an agent and talent scout, discovering such actors as Howard Keel and Rhonda Fleming.

She had a distinct talent for being able to spot future movie stars, and she definitely saw potential in Norma Jeane. However, before anything further could be done, the young model travelled to Las Vegas to obtain her divorce from Dougherty.

While the trip was the beginning of her future as a single woman, it was also stressful in various ways, due to several bouts of illness, one of which put her in hospital for a time. Miss Snively and Joyce Ryan wrote about the experience in their notes:

This was a lonely period in her life. Norma Jeane had very few close friends. She was always friendly with the other models and the photographers but she never went out socially with them. Miss Snively became more than an employer – Norma Jeane felt she could trust and confide in her. During the long six weeks waiting period, she received many tear-stained letters. However, the one she remembers best was written during one of the happy times. There was a western movie being made and Norma Jeane had gone to watch the shooting. The crew was as attracted to the beautiful girl as she to them. They invited her to have lunch with them and she met Roy Rogers. Norma Jeane loved horses and was more attracted to Trigger than Roy Rogers. She was allowed to ride Trigger – 'Cross my heart I did' she wrote to Miss Snively. After shooting was completed, she was invited for dinner. As she left with the crew she was asked for her autograph. 'I tried to tell them I wasn't in the movie, but they wouldn't believe me so I signed their books.' I wonder if that fan realizes he has the first autograph of Marilyn Monroe/Norma Jeane.

'the young model travelled to Las Vegas to obtain her divorce from Dougherty'

The letter Miss Snively refers to was written on 25 May 1946. As well as reporting on Roy Rogers, the young model expressed what a colourful town Las Vegas was but explained that she had also felt lonely for home. She asked Miss Snively to write back with news of Los Angeles and gave her regards to Miss Snively's mother, Myrtle, and tutor, Miss Smith. Photographers mentioned in the letter include Paul Parry,

While Norma Jeane was in Las Vegas she wrote a long letter to Miss Snively, sharing all her news. (From the archive of Ben and Astrid Franse)

604½ South 3rd St.
Las Vegas, Nev.
May 25th 1946

Dear Miss Snively,

I'm having lots of rest and I'm getting tan. Its very warm and honestly the sun shines all the time.

Las Vegas is really a colossal town with the Helldorado celebration and all. It lasted for five days, they had rodeos and parades everyday.

Roy Rogers was in town making a picture. I met him, and rode his horse "Trigger" (cross my heart I did!) What a horse!

I was walking down the street one day last week and noticed they were shooting a movie so like everyone else I stood and watched. In between shootings a couple of fellows

from Republic Studio walked
over to me and asked me
if I would please come over
and meet some actor (I don't
remember his name.) I think
his last name was Crosby or
something like that.) Anyway
he wanted to meet me and
did and I met most of the
studio people including Roy Rogers
and I rode his horse, ga he
is nice.

They asked me to have dinner
with them at the Last Frontier
and then we went to the
rodeo. What a day! Ever since
I've been signing autograph
books and cowboy-boy hats...
When I try to tell them
I'm not in pictures they t
I'm just trying to avoi
signing their books, so
them.

They've gone now. Its g
lonely here in Las Vegas...

*Marilyn's letter to Miss Snively. (From the
archive of Ben and Astrid Franse)*

certainly a wild town.

Miss Snively, I would love
to hear from you and hear
whats new.

Please give my best regards
to Mrs. Snively and Miss Smith.
Also to Dick Miller if you see
him. I hope has been able to
sell some of those pictures, he
is so nice.

Is John Randolph and Paul
Parry back in town yet?
How is Mr. Bloom? I wonder if
Eclston agency is ever going
to pay me? Do you ever hear
from Mr. Wellingh about me?
I didn't know six weeks
could pass so slowly.

I will write again soon.

Love,

Norma Jeane.

John Randolph, Hal Bloom and Laszlo Willinger. She wonders if Parry and Randolph are back in town and asks if Willinger ever speaks to Miss Snively about her. Richard Miller is also mentioned – Norma Jeane asks the agency boss to say hello to him and hopes he has been able to sell some of the shots he took of her. 'He is so nice,' she wrote in the letter.

The next reported contact between agent and client was on 2 July, when Norma Jeane sent a telegram to tell Miss Snively that she was currently in hospital with measles. She apologised for the delay in writing but promised to be in touch again soon. On the back of the correspondence, the agency boss wrote a note which seems to confirm that, despite the fact that she wasn't supposed to be working while awaiting the divorce, Norma Jeane did do the odd modelling job: 'Contrary to the plot of *How To Marry A Millionaire* [a film Marilyn made in 1953] this telegram shows it is Marilyn rather than [co-star] Betty Grable that has the measles … and on a location modelling job in Las Vegas.'

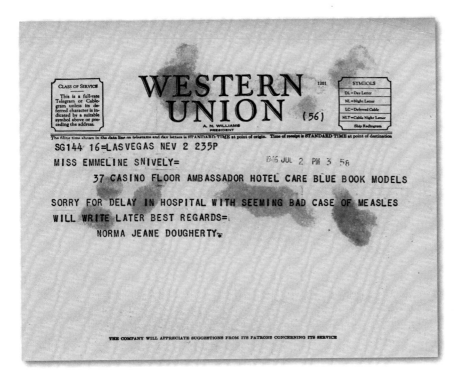

Marilyn's telegram to Miss Snively. (From the archive of Ben and Astrid Franse)

FIVE

WHO IS THE GIRL ON *LAFF*?

Before Norma Jeane finally returned to California in July 1946, Miss Snively was hard at work trying to further both Norma Jeane's acting and modelling career. She had appeared on a copy of *Laff* magazine, and as a result she gained the attention of producer Howard Hughes, who was in hospital recovering from a plane crash. 'I received a phone call from Mr Hughes, asking who the girl was on the cover of *Laff*,' wrote Miss Snively. 'I phoned Louella Parsons and Hedda Hopper who picked up the item and gave Norma Jeane her first coast to coast publicity.' By the time she returned to California, Hughes had either lost interest or was not in a position to sign Norma Jeane after all, but she was still eager to continue with her career. The notes in the archive related to this period, say:

[Helen Ainsworth] took Norma Jeane to Twentieth Century Fox, where she arranged a screen test in colour. The results were wonderful and she was signed to a starlet's contract for a salary and training in the studio workshops. Ben Lyon took an interest in Norma Jeane and chose the name Marilyn for her. When he asked if there was a last name she particularly liked, she said yes – her grandmother's last name had been Monroe. 'Mmmmarilyn Mmmmonroe, yes I like the way that sounds,' Marilyn said. And so it was …

Ben Lyon remembered the historic meeting between himself and the budding actress, and he made mention of it during an interview for an unknown newspaper the day after Marilyn's death. 'She walked into my office in California one day in 1946. She was beautiful. I saw right away that she had the makings of a great star and gave her a contract. She was thrilled to death,' he said.

Marilyn standing on some steps for a Fox publicity photo that was taken at the beginning of her film career. (From the collection of Bill Pursel)

'It must be remembered,' wrote Miss Snively, 'that Marilyn had no dramatic training. All she had with her were clippings from her commercial modelling jobs, her magazine covers and several colour transparencies which photographers had loaned her along with their best wishes … That story that she was discovered as a babysitter for some director just isn't true. I've heard all kinds of rumours about her start, but they're not true; she's not that kind of girl.'

The babysitting story was revealed soon after the signing of the Twentieth Century Fox contract. It was used by many newspapers as an example of how it is often better to be in the right place at the right time rather than to go to drama school or work on stage. The story was completely false, of course, but that still didn't stop publicity photos being taken of the young starlet in charge of several young babies. Marilyn later revealed that it was the studio that told her to spread the babysitting story to all who would listen, 'though it strictly wasn't true. You'd think that they would have used a little more imagination and have had me at least a daddy sitter!'

While Marilyn was supported in her career choice by her foster mother, Aunt Ana, and several friends, one person who did not approve was her mother, Gladys. She had been in a psychiatric home for quite some time but had returned to California and was currently living with her daughter and Aunt Ana. Gladys had never been a supportive part of Marilyn's life, but now that she was in close proximity, she felt the need to give her opinion on everything she was doing, particularly her new-found acting career.

The older woman was outwardly critical, refusing to take any interest whatsoever in her daughter's screen contract and walking away when the conversation was

Marilyn poses outside her home in 1946. She later gave this photo to her friend Bill Pursel. Unknown photographer. (From the collection of Bill Pursel)

brought up. When Marilyn started doing voice exercises and studying her reflection in the mirror, Gladys would call the whole thing ridiculous and question why she wasn't doing something more productive with her life. No amount of persuasion from family members would get her to change her mind over what she deemed to be a disgraceful waste of time.

Surprisingly, however, Gladys did give a little attention to the subject of Marilyn's modelling career and actually travelled to the Ambassador Hotel at one point to meet Miss Snively.

The mother thanked the agency boss for what she had done for Marilyn, though unfortunately no more light can be shed on the historic meeting, as, apart from confirming that she met Gladys and Aunt Ana, Miss Snively gives no other details in the archive.

Cars seemed to play a big role when it came to Marilyn's amateur modelling career. Unknown photographer. (From the collection of Michelle Morgan and Bill Pursel)

Marilyn's half-sister, Berniece Baker Miracle, wrote about her sibling's modelling career in her book *My Sister Marilyn* and described a day when the two travelled together to the Ambassador Hotel. The idea was that the young actress would introduce Berniece to Miss Snively and then afterwards the two girls would have lunch in the restaurant. However, while the day was enjoyable, it also turned into something of a confessional.

Whilst sitting in the hotel, Marilyn told her sister that she had something she wanted to speak about and then confessed to having been photographed nude. No mention was made of the photographer, but it was undoubtedly Earl Moran, who had taken the somewhat risqué snaps just a short time before. Marilyn's biggest fear was that her foster mother, Aunt Ana, would find out about them, but it would seem that her worries were in the end unfounded.

*An unusual photo
– possibly an early
Fox publicity picture –
showing Marilyn lying
in a haystack with a
large hat next to her.
Unknown photographer.
(From the collection of
Bill Pursel)*

The only nude photos that appeared in the years ahead were released several years after her foster mother's death.

Marilyn loved her time at Twentieth Century Fox and would travel every day to the studio to see if there were any castings and to take part in the various classes that were made available to her. Miss Snively believed that the numerous lessons she took were a result of feeling as though the educational side of her life had been somewhat neglected:

> She has always believed in work, believed so much in fact that unwittingly she antagonized several of the more jealous girls who were in studio classes with her. They just couldn't believe that any beginner was willing to work as hard as Marilyn did in order to get ahead. Marilyn did everything she was told to do at the studio. She devoured every crumb of instruction. Usually late to most functions, she was the first to attend classes and the last to leave.

During the course of a year at Fox, Marilyn was cast in two movies: *Dangerous Years* and *Scudda Hoo! Scudda Hay!* Sadly, however, she

had virtually nothing to do in either of them. In the former she played the small role of a waitress, though when it was released she was barely mentioned in the cast lists and no details of her performance were included in the reviews. That was probably just as well, as it barely raised an eyebrow with most critics. *The Film Daily* described it as 'minor scale stuff that limps along. It contributes little to the sphere of dramatic entertainment.' The *Film Bulletin* pulled no punches when it declared *Dangerous Years* to be 'too incredible and full of obvious hokum for most audiences ... Its direction and writing is strongly reminiscent of a radio soap opera.'

In *Scudda Hoo! Scudda Hay!* Marilyn's role was, for the most part, cut out, though, contrary to popular belief, she was still credited (albeit last) on the cast list. Critical responses were fairly lukewarm by the time of release, though the *Showmen's Trade Review* did say it was 'wholesome entertainment for the entire family and should do good business on the strength of its cast names'. No mention was made of Marilyn's almost non-existent part, but young actress Natalie Wood was described as excellent as June Haver's 'snooping young brat of a sister'.

While *Scudda Hoo! Scudda Hay!* and *Dangerous Years* were never going to give Marilyn any acting awards or increase her profile, they did give her a degree of experience in front of a movie camera. Another positive thing to come from the roles was a portfolio of publicity photos designed to raise interest in the young starlet. One such picture, showing Marilyn pretending to play tennis, was sent from Fox to various newspapers around the country. In it she was described as a girl who was once called the 'Oomph Girl' at school and was now known as the 'Mmmmmm Girl' of movies. It was something of an exaggeration, but it did earn valuable exposure for the newly discovered actress.

Opposite: Marilyn posing in a floral bikini, possibly a Fox publicity photo. (From the collection of Dionne Abraham)

A scantily dressed Marilyn at the eighteenth hole of a golf course, in what is possibly an early Fox publicity photo. Unknown photographer. (From the collection of Bill Pursel)

Despite now being a fully fledged starlet, Marilyn was still a down-to-earth girl, as Miss Snively later commented on. 'Unlike several other girls I know, the screen contract did not go to her head. She was the same sweet, un-assuming girl she had always been.' With that in mind, she continued to model whenever she could, and Miss Snively kept her in mind for any jobs that came up. Such an opportunity happened in late summer/early autumn of 1946.

> 'She was the same sweet, un-assuming girl she had always been'

There was a group of amateur photographers in Los Angeles who would often go out on the road to take photos of their local surroundings. Group 13, as Miss Snively called them, wanted Marilyn to be their model. The agency boss secured her availability, and then they all met at Miss Snively's house on Wilshire Boulevard, before travelling to Big Tujunga Creek (or Big Tujunga River as Miss Snively called it in the archive) for a photo session. It would seem that the group was well known to the agency boss, who wrote in her notes, 'Amateur photographers in Group 13 used to start girls on their way to stardom [and supply] free photos.' In turn they received a great deal of experience photographing the model in various different environments, whilst under the expert instruction of Fred William Carter.

Carter, a well-respected artist and photographer, had been associated with several members of the group for some years. Phillip Sampson, a Group 13 devotee and doctor from Los Angeles, was one of his photographic students and would often invite Carter to speak at various talks and meetings he held in the area. Sampson, it should be noted, was also one of the people invited to photograph Marilyn on the day of the river shoot. As well as giving lectures on the art of photography, Carter also often held photograph exhibitions in the Los Angeles area. Three years before the 1946 trip, he displayed a variety of war photos in the Central library; just a few months after the shoot, pieces of his past work were on show in a Santa Monica exhibition. He was also called upon to judge several modelling competitions over the years, so his experience in the area of photographing people was second-to-none.

Opposite: Marilyn — casually dressed in a T-shirt and rolled-up jeans — leans across the bonnet of a Cadillac whilst on a field trip, photographer: Richard Whiteman. (From the archive of Ben and Astrid Franse)

NUMBER   PAGE

DATE *after Fox Contract*   LOCATION *Big tujunga River Field trip*

EVENT *Field trip*

OTHER PEOPLE

PHOTOGRAPHER *Dick Whiteman*   *No Release*

Comments *Miss Snively titled this " Wishfull Thinking " sitting on the hood of W L Gilberts (the criminal lawyer) Cadillac She was newly under contract to 20th + didn't have a car like this of her own yet —*

Miss Snively kept notes about many of Marilyn's modelling jobs. Here she writes about the field trip to Big Tujunga Creek. (From the archive of Ben and Astrid Franse)

On the day of the Tujunga shoot, one of the photographic students, William Gilbert – an attorney from Los Angeles – drove his Cadillac to the location. One of the first photos taken that day was of Marilyn wearing jeans and a striped T-shirt, sitting happily on the hood of the car. Miss Snively called the shot 'Wishful Thinking' and wrote in her notes, 'She was newly under contract to Twentieth and didn't have a car like this of her own yet.'

Once the photograph was taken, Marilyn changed into a bathing costume, which Miss Snively said had been bought wholesale for her, and then waded into the creek, where she was photographed by members of the group. Miss Snively's notes are at times hard to read, but the photographers present on that fateful day appear to be: Richard 'Dick' Whiteman, artist; William Gilbert, attorney; Phillip Sampson, doctor; Joe Gilbert, gas company president; Dan C. Hickson; and Jack Lanager. They were watched over by a young boy called Ernie, who appears to have come with the group for a fun day out.

The photographs taken during the shoot are incredible, due mainly to the fact that they were taken in a location vary rarely seen in any other Marilyn photographs. There are countless photos of the starlet

Opposite: Dressed in a bathing costume, Marilyn poses on some rocks by Big Tujunga Creek during a photo shooot. Photographer: Richard Whiteman. (From the archive of Ben and Astrid Franse)

NUMBER   PAGE
DATE   1946   LOCATION
                      Big Tujunga River
EVENT
        Field trip for Club 13 amateur cands —

OTHER PEOPLE

PHOTOGRAPHER Dick Whitman   no release
Comments These Trees died too + before the
          flood in the canyon —
                Beautiful in her Dawn of Hollywood
        2 piece B Suit — I purchased wholesale for her

at the beach, poolside or in fields and general countryside, but to see her knee-deep in a creek or balanced on large river rocks is a rare treat indeed. In her notes, Miss Snively writes that Marilyn was a hit with everyone at the session: 'She was most cooperative, and kept up the spirits of the expedition with her sunny personality, despite the lack of California sunshine.' This is certainly apparent when looking at the resulting photos, which show that it didn't matter where the photographers wanted her to stand, Marilyn was more than willing to do it.

'Marilyn was a hit with everyone at the session'

Until now, it has always been thought that the only photos of Marilyn and Miss Snively together were taken on the set of *There's No Business Like Show Business*, when she came to see her former student in action. With the discovery of the Blue Book archive, however, we can now see that they were photographed some eight years before that. While Marilyn is perched on a rock, in the distance is the lone figure of Miss Snively, sitting almost un-noticed on the other side of the creek. Holding her knees, and wearing a scarf on her head, the agency boss is not looking in Marilyn's direction but instead seems lost in her own thoughts. Notes related to this photograph read 'Miss Snively in background of MM in her two-piece bathing suit ... Pretty steep competition for E Snively.'

Another fascinating shot shows Marilyn looking at the camera of Dick Whiteman, while amateur photographer William Gilbert is snapping her from another angle. Miss Snively liked the unusual aspect of this particular photograph so much that she made two notes about it. The first said the following:

Marilyn was always a good sport and really enjoyed modelling, as can be seen as she tries to pose for two photographers at the same time, and shooting from different directions, too. Posing for several cameras and trying to give them all your best angles is no easy feat and a challenge to the most professional models. Marlene Dietrich stands out as a subject who can handle herself with many photographers shooting from many angles, as well as anyone. Marilyn is taking direction here from members of the Group 13 amateur pictorialists of Los Angeles.

10

1946

Amateur Photographers GROUP I3,booked model Norma Jean Dougherty,now known as Marilyn Monroe for a field trip to the Big Tijunga River.She was most cooperative, and kept up the spirits of the expedition with her sunny personality, despite the lack of California sunshine.

#117

Photo by
Richard Whiteman

Blue Book Models
617 SO. VERMONT AVE.
DUNKIRK 2-8043

Miss Snively's notes on the back of a field trip photo. (From the archive of Ben and Astrid Franse)

The second note, written on a worksheet, described the photograph as 'Natural Beauty. Nature and a lovely woman. Build a dam and see the reflections in the water. Marilyn tugs at some growing roots to make a better picture. No wonder deer came down the hill in the background to drink the water – such a secluded spot. Mr Gilbert is wearing trunks of course. He got a close-up this time.'

Two more photos in the archive show Marilyn once again balanced on rocks beside the river. The third one, however, is slightly different and shows the young actress beside a large tree, her head turned slightly away from the camera.

NUMBER

PAGE

DATE after 20th
Century Fox

LOCATION
Big Tujunga

EVENT Field Trip at Big Tujunga River

OTHER PEOPLE Amateur photogs from group 13
were there. Dick Whitman Artist Dan Hickson
Cu & Gilbert attorney Pres General Lens
Do " Gas Co Pres of S M - Studio

PHOTOGRAPHER Dick Whitman no release
Comments Miss Snively in background & M M
in her 2 piece B suit from Diary of Hollywood
Pretty deep competition for E Snively.

Wading through the creek, Marilyn looks into the camera of one photographer, whilst another snaps her from a different angle – a photograph Miss Snively particuarly liked. Photographer: Richard Whiteman. (From the archive of Ben and Astrid Franse)

Marilyn was always a good sport and really enjoyed modeling, as can be seen as she tries to pose for two photographers at the same time, and shooting from different directions too. Posing for several cameras and trying to give them all your best angles is no easy feat and a challenge to the most professional models.

Marlene Deitrich stands out as a subject who can handle herself with many photographers shooting from many angles, as well as anyone.

Marilyn is taking direction here from mebers of "Group 13" amateur pictorialsts. of Los Angeles

Richard Whiteman Photo

Miss Snively's notes on the back of a field trip photo. (From the archive of Ben and Astrid Franse)

Opposite: Marilyn perched on a rock, taking centre stage, with the lone figure of Miss Snively in the background. Photographer: Richard Whiteman. (From the archive of Ben and Astrid Franse)

Opposite: More smiles
for the camera as
Marilyn leans against
the rocks of Big Tujunga
Creek during the field
trip. Photographer:
Richard Whiteman.
(From the archive of Ben
and Astrid Franse)

Field trip record sheet.
(From the archive of Ben
and Astrid Franse)

All of these shots were packed away by Miss Snively and have never been seen again until now.

Although the session may not have been professional in nature, nor taken by a famous photographer or artist, the photos taken that day at Tujunga are unique and important for various reasons. They not only give light to what it must have been like for the photography students and model on the trip, but they also show just how happy Marilyn was to be taking part. At the very beginning of her screen career she was contented and looking forward to the future, and this is clear to see on her face. Although Miss Snively chose never to release the pictures, she held both the session and Tujunga Creek in great affection. She wrote about it several times in her notes and years later scribbled, 'This lovely spot is all gone now. Trees and rocks all [washed away] with the 1966 flood.'

> 'All of these shots were packed away by Miss Snively and have never been seen again until now'

Another amateur photographer to use Marilyn as a model – this time in a motion picture – was Leo Caloia. Caloia had started to make home movies when he was just 19 and quickly progressed to

working for Paramount, where he was employed for a time in the 1930s. Eventually he left the industry altogether but continued his interest, taking motion pictures of many film stars on the red carpet, including Charlie Chaplin, Mary Pickford and Gary Cooper. In 1946, however, he was given the chance of filming an up-and-coming star, though, of course, he did not know this at the time.

The opportunity came when Caloia took part in the KFI Radio Station Camera Clinic program in 1946. These kinds of workshops were something that happened every week at the Ambassador Hotel, and were similar in style to the Group 13 photography trips that Miss Snively helped to arrange. The only difference was that this time the girls would move around the pool area and various other parts of the hotel while amateur and budding film-makers used their motion-picture cameras to record the activities.

Travelling to the hotel with his wife Frances, Caloia was introduced to Marilyn and six other models, who were all posing on stage. He then began filming while the audience discussed the various techniques involved. Footage of his time with Marilyn shows the model in the same swimsuit she had worn for the Group 13 photographs, moving slowly in a circle while occasionally flicking her hair, crossing her legs and talking to the camera. This natural awareness was something that impressed Caloia to a great degree, especially as there had been no rehearsal or practice run before shooting began.

While he enjoyed filming Marilyn, Caloia could be forgiven for thinking the event was nothing out of the ordinary. It wasn't until some years later that he realised how much history had been made that day. Caloia later discussed the experience of working with the Blue Book Agency in a rare interview, telling the journalist that if a girl had talent in the entertainment business then Miss Snively was able to draw it out. He also revealed his first thoughts on meeting Marilyn: 'One girl was particularly very cooperative, and just wanted to do anything I said, like I was a big-time director, but I was a nobody … She was a very pleasant, nice, warm-hearted girl.'

Opposite: Marilyn balances on a rock during the Big Tujunga Creek field trip. Photographer: Richard Whiteman. (From the archive of Ben and Astrid Franse)

Close-up of Norma Jeane. Photographer: Leo Caloia. (From the archive of Ben and Astrid Franse)

Opposite, top: Norma Jeane in a bikini. Photographer: Leo Caloia. Opposite, bottom: Leo Caloia filming Norma Jeane. (From the archive of Ben and Astrid Franse)

Although Caloia never went into professional film-making, he was always well respected for his movies of Marilyn and other stars. He was a member of the Los Angeles Cinema club and in the 1970s became a charter member of the Orange County Cinematographers. There he wowed fellow members with his camera skills and his tales of Hollywood and, of course, Marilyn. He would remain wonderfully proud of the footage of her, until his death in 2001.

While Miss Snively never believed in Marilyn's ability to make it in fashion modelling, the young actress occasionally took on jobs anyway and actually took part in a full-blown show at the Ambassador in the summer of 1946. Miss Snively wrote about the experience in her notes: 'She came back to our studio and we gave her some free brush-up advice in fashion modelling. I saw that fashion show, and do you know something? She was still a lousy fashion model.'

Opposite: Marilyn modelling a dress for a fashion show. Photographer: Larry Kronquist.

Marilyn proves that she is just as self-assured as the other fashion models in this shot taken for a fashion show held at the Ambassador Hotel. Photographer: Larry Kronquist. (Both images, the archive of Ben and Astrid Franse)

While she was never going to be a catwalk sensation, perhaps calling Marilyn lousy was a tad unfair. Amateur moviemaker Leo Caloia was at the Ambassador that day and actually filmed the young woman modelling clothes around the pool area, and photographer Larry Kronquist took photographs. Caloia's video footage can now be viewed freely online and shows Marilyn wearing a blue dress and cork-heeled shoes, walking around the pool area with several other models. She is filmed talking, sitting, posing and smiling. The video demonstrates that the other models were no better or worse than she was, and at times she actually seems much more assured than some of the women with her.

The same applies to the photographs taken by Larry Kronquist, where Marilyn again stands out as one of the better-poised young women. On the back of one photograph showing five models, Miss Snively wrote the following note: 'Fashion show line up at Ambassador pool includes Marilyn second from the left. She wore a ten skirt and a size twelve top.' Another shot by Kronquist shows Marilyn alone, still modelling the same dress, and standing next to a wall. The photos confirm that while she may not have been the height of a professional fashion model, the young woman could certainly pose successfully in a dress. Interestingly, while Miss Snively did not think much of Marilyn's talent in that direction, her dedication to the young model meant that she forever kept her fashion photographs neatly tucked away in her archive.

'Marilyn again stands out as one of the better poised young women'

* * *

A Christmas Parade was held in December 1946, and Marilyn was asked to appear on the Alan Young float. Mr Young was a radio star turned actor, who later became popular in his role as Wilbur Post in the television show *Mister Ed*. For now, however, he was famous for his radio work, and it was in that capacity that he came to be introduced to Marilyn. Working as a starlet at Fox, the actress was still eager to take part not only in modelling jobs but also publicity appearances, so when she was approached by Ben Lyon to appear on the float, she was very happy to comply.

Joe Jasgur came back into Marilyn's life briefly on the evening of the parade by taking a photograph of the float, complete with everyone on board. Miss Snively added the photograph to her file and on the back noted the following: 'Norma Jeane (Marilyn) wears a white sweater and carries a banner with other Fox starlets on a float in the Santa Clause Parade on Hollywood Boulevard.'

In the 2012 book *Marilyn Monroe: Private and Undisclosed*, Alan Young recalled his memories of the evening with author Michelle Morgan:

NUMBER
DATE 1948   PAGE
                            LOCATION
EVENT   Hollywood Blvd – Holly
        Santa Clause Parade
OTHER PEOPLE
        Other Starlets at Fox
PHOTOGRAPHER Joe Jasgur
COMMENTS   Norma Jean (Marilyn) wears a white
    sweater & carries a banner with other Fox starlett
    on a float in the Santa Clause Parade on Hollywood
                                    Blud at the
                                    Xmas

"Santa Claus Lane" Where Movie Stars shop. Hollywood, Cal.

Marilyn took part in the annual Hollywood Santa Claus parade in 1946. This photo shows an aerial view of a typical parade, taken in the mid- to late 1940s. Unknown photographer. (Photograph from the collection of Michelle Morgan, worksheet from the archive of Ben and Astrid Franse).

After the parade we went to the Brown Derby, but I didn't drink and neither did Norma Jeane, so we decided instead to go and get some cocoa together … She seemed like a frightened rabbit at first, and I didn't realize she had been raised without parents. I really liked her.

The idea of the Fox contract providing Marilyn with a whole host of acting jobs was thwarted in 1947, as Marilyn later explained to reporter Liza Wilson, saying, 'I did pin-ups and cheesecake at the studio after [*Scudda Hoo! Scudda Hay!*], but I never had another go at acting.' Instead, they continued to use her in a whole host of publicity photos, including modelling a bustle swimsuit, named after the gathering of material on the bottom area.

'This outfit is not recommended for energetic swimming'

Made from ivory silk and boasting red roses and green leaves, some articles came with a warning that, 'This outfit is not recommended for

A fun picture of Marilyn with skis for a Fox publicity photo. (From the collection of Bill Pursel)

energetic swimming.' Various versions of the photograph were distributed, each one showing Marilyn posing happily with the ruffles firmly on display. One newspaper even described the clothing as something that had been specifically designed for the actress by studio wardrobe director Charles LeMaire, after she had surprised everyone by receiving a huge amount of fan mail. Other photographs released around this time showed the actress playing and posing on the beach with a rather talented spaniel named Ruffles. Newspapers described the dog as being 'guest of honour at a beach picnic staged by Marilyn Monroe, a youthful newcomer to the ranks of film players'. Yet another set showed her in a series of rather eccentric but fun poses, dressed in a bikini, wearing skis in a beach-like setting.

As well as pictures, a great many appearances were planned to bring publicity for both herself and Twentieth Century Fox. One such event was held in April 1947, and saw her travelling to the Hollywood Legion Stadium with seventeen other starlets so she could take part in the Annual Ceremony and Presentation of Honorary Colonels. The event did not raise her profile much, but she did apparently receive a badge of honour, as did the other actresses in attendance.

She also visited a store in Salinas for a publicity appearance and found herself so popular that the shop owner ran out of photographs and had to order more as quickly as possible. Her journey to the event was not in any way glamorous or even comfortable. In the 2010 book *Fragments*, by Bernard Comment and Stanley Buchthal, Marilyn's

Marilyn lying happily on a beach with Ruffles the dog beside her, taken for a Fox publicity photo shoot. The shadow of the photographer can be seen in the foreground. (From the collection of Bill Pursel)

Marilyn with friends at the Las Vegas Flamingo Hotel. She was employed for the weekend as a model, and to entice punters to the gambling tables. Unknown photographer. (From the collection of Dionne Abraham)

thoughts were revealed through her private notebook. In the text she writes about the uncomfortable journey to the venue, travelling for hours on a crowded bus, falling asleep and hoping she wasn't about to lean on the young man next to her. Her notes also covered various other passengers on the bus and show that no matter how successful her modelling career was, at that point in time Twentieth Century Fox thought of her as nothing but yet another starlet.

Another appearance Marilyn was asked to take part in meant going even further afield, this time to the newly opened Flamingo Hotel in Las Vegas. The hotel was so glamorous that it had even flown in palm trees from Australia, rather than use ones available from California. It was a talking point with guests and media alike, and columnist

Erskine Johnson described the complex as looking just like an MGM movie set. It came equipped with specially designed wallpaper, handmade leather wastepaper baskets and four $12 designer ashtrays in each room. Celebrities flocked there on a regular basis, and, within weeks of opening, the hotel had played host to The Andrews Sisters and Abbott and Costello. 'It's all so swanky' Johnson told his readers in March 1947.

Eager to make their own mark on the hotel, in summer 1947 Twentieth Century Fox sent some of their starlets – including Marilyn – to make publicity appearances in the ballroom and pose for photographs. Once there, the young woman was also required to play at the various gambling tables (with casino money) so as to entice and encourage punters to try their hands at the games themselves. The job wasn't the most thrilling or glamorous, but she took it in her stride. Only one photograph exists of the event and shows Marilyn standing next to the famed Australian palm trees, with some actors and other starlets.

At the Brentwood Country Club on 20 July, Marilyn made an appearance in support of the annual Fox golf tournament, and then on 17 August she was chosen to be a golf caddy for another competition, this time at Cheviot Hills. There does not appear to have been much press done for the event, but another celebrity tournament was held just a few weeks earlier at the California Country Club, which gives an idea of the kind of occasion it was. No articles mention that Marilyn was in attendance on that particular day, but she may well have been, as a number of starlets were there to act as scorers for the celebrities playing golf. Famous faces included Marilyn's idol Clark Gable, along with Bob Hope, Jack Benny, John Carroll and Benny Goodman.

The mention of actor John Carroll is interesting because Marilyn was to meet him at the Cheviot Hills event just weeks later. At that particular tournament, she was assigned to look after him and his golfing partners, and Carroll immediately took a great interest in the actress and her career. Away from the publicity appearance, the two struck up a friendship, and very quickly she became an acting client of his wife, Lucille Ryman.

While there is no doubt that publicity appearances and photo shoots kept Marilyn busy during her time at Twentieth Century Fox, unfortunately neither were enough to ensure she be kept under contract. 'When option time came I was dropped,' she said. Later the actress described how she immediately went to see Studio Head Darryl F. Zanuck, who Marilyn said had not introduced himself to her the whole time she was at the studio. Her intention was to ask why she had been dropped, but his secretary fobbed her off by explaining he had left the office and gone to Sun Valley. His refusal to see anything worthwhile in the actress was not a temporary thing. Even when she returned to the studio in the years ahead, Zanuck would never understand the attention Marilyn received – the two were never destined to become friends.

Opposite: Marilyn playing golf. Unknown photographer. (From the collection of Bill Pursel)

SIX

MMMMARILYN MMMMONROE

In the weeks following the dropped contract, Marilyn was understandably devastated, but at the same time she knew that it was all part of the Hollywood game. 'I think if other girls know how bad I was when I started, they'll be encouraged,' she said. 'I finally made up my mind I wanted to be an actress, and I was not going to let my lack of confidence ruin my chances.' Instead of moping, she went back to modelling, often working with photographers she had met through the Blue Book Agency. Earl Moran was a regular, and she continued to pose for his calendar photos for some time to come.

Another job came up either just before or after being dropped from Fox, and it called upon Marilyn to model two swimsuits for *Holiday* magazine. The photographs were eventually used in the February 1948 issue, which mistakenly said that Marilyn was still signed to Fox. In the advert it declared, 'New fabrics as well as styles are important in the 1948 bathing suits.' The photographs accompanying the article showed Marilyn once again poolside. In one she is wearing a white all-in-one suit made from elasticated matelassé taffeta, while the other has a bow-tie-style bra that separated the top from the bottom, therefore giving the illusion of a bikini.

In terms of her acting career, Marilyn decided that if a studio was ever going to sign her to another contract, she should delve further into her studies as an actress. With that in mind she undertook various acting lessons and also became involved with the Bliss-Hayden theatre, where she acted in a play called *Glamour Preferred*, from 12 October to 2 November. The part didn't earn Marilyn any mentions in the national press, but the next Bliss-Hayden appearance – in the play *Penny Wise* – did. While nothing else is known about her work in the production, the *Los Angeles Times* reported that rehearsals were underway on 5 December, with an expected opening date of shortly before Christmas.

It wasn't all work that was mentioned in the columns, however; Marilyn's love life certainly seems to have been a source of some entertainment too. In September 1947, Louella Parsons reported that the starlet was dating Alice Faye's brother Charlie, and the two were frequently seen at the Seacombers venue in Malibu. Columnist Jimmy Fidler wrote a rather amusing story of Marilyn dining at the Mocambo nightclub in December 1947, where she became friendly with a young man by the name of Steve Crane.

Lila Leeds, another Bliss-Hayden actress who had also appeared in a few films, saw what was going on and became insanely jealous. According to Fidler, she marched Marilyn away from Crane, before swinging wildly at him in a jealous rage. Whether or not either story had any truth is not known. What we do know, however, is that Miss Snively tipped off columnists including Louella Parsons and Hedda Hopper about her client's venture into films in 1946. With the Fox contract over she had returned to modelling and it is a distinct possibility that the agency boss was trying to find other ways of keeping Marilyn's name in the limelight.

While modelling to pay her bills, Marilyn was thrilled to be given another studio contract, this time with Columbia Pictures. She recalled this particular time in her life during a 1953 article for *Filmland* magazine:

I had had a contract for a year at Twentieth Century Fox but I felt that didn't count because I had played only one small role which was finally cut out of the picture. But the Columbia contract was different. I was sure that my big opportunity had come.

9. Marilyn with Mexican hats.
Photographer: Laszlo Willinger.
(From the archive of Ben and
Astrid Franse)

Marilyn Monroe

11. *Marilyn sitting on the beach. Photographer: Laszlo Willinger. (From the archive of Ben and Astrid Franse)*

Opposite: 10. Marilyn in striped bathing suit. Photographer: possibly Laszlo Willinger. (From the collection of Kim Goodwin)

12. *Marilyn in red bathing suit. Photographer: possibly Laszlo Willinger. (From the collection of Kim Goodwin)*

BLUE BOOK MODELS *39 Casino Floor · Ambassador Hotel · Los Angeles 5, California*

* AVAILABLE FOR FASHION, PHOTOGRAPHY, ILLUSTRATION AND MOTION PICTURE *

FOR IMMEDIATE RELEASE (WITH ART) DATE-
(DUPLICATE)

Room 962
Chamber
Commerce Bldg

BLUE BOOK MODEL: NORMA JEAN DOUGHERTY proves to
be California Model Extraordinary, by appearing on 5
National Magazine Covers in one month.

NORMA JEAN is a healthy Product of the San
Fernando Valley.

VITAL STATISTICS:

Height- 5'6"
Weight- 120 lbs.
Bust-   36
Waist-   24
Hips-   34
~~Woof shoot~~

Light hair and blue eyes and a beautiful smile.
What more could you want?

She is curently gracing the covers of:

THE FAMILY CIRCLE
LAFF
U.S. CAMERA with CAROL LANDIS
PAGEANT
SALUTE

~~WE SALUTE YOU NORMA JEAN!~~

For Every Blue Book Model, Dial Drexel 7316

13. Blue Book press release about Marilyn's covers. (From the archive of Ben and Astrid Franse)

New fabrics as well as styles are important in the 1948 bathing suits

Untarnishable silver thread woven into a diamond pattern shines in this white elasticized matelassé taffeta. The suit, worn by Marilyn Monroe of 20th Century Fox, is a one-piece classic with specially constructed bra.
CALTEX OF CALIFORNIA

Marilyn Monroe basks in a one-piece swim suit. It is made of soft velvet treated chemically for water-repellency (an example of new swim fabrics). The bow-tie bra and shirred trunks are separated for two-piece effect.
COLE OF CALIFORNIA

14. Holiday Magazine advert with bikinis. Unknown photographer. (From the collection of Ben and Astrid Franse, and also Eric Patry)

15. *Marilyn at a New York pool. Unknown photographer. (From the collection of Ben and Astrid Franse)*

16. Publicity photo showing Marilyn in a yellow sweater and pink scarf. Photographer: John Miehle. (From the collection of Michelle Morgan)

MARILYN MONROE

17. *This publicity photo shows Norma Jeane's complete transformation into superstar Marilyn Monroe. (From the collection of Michelle Morgan)*

The studio sent out short articles to various newspapers across the country, telling reporters that Marilyn was a happy starlet who had just won a contract to make pictures. Whereas Fox had previously told the media that she had been discovered while babysitting, Columbia went one better and announced that she had been a top model working in New York before they had discovered her. The fact that she was really working for a smaller agency in the heart of Hollywood was not glamorous enough for the studio, it would seem.

Around this time, Marilyn was sent to pose for various headshots and publicity photos, just as she had done while working at Fox. Some of these shots are easy to spot and are in the same vein as many other star shots of the 1940s, but several rather mysterious photos were also taken by a gentleman called John Miehle. Miehle had worked as a still photographer and assistant cameraman since the 1920s, and in about 1948 he took two beautiful colour shots of Marilyn, showing her wearing a yellow sweater and dark-pink scarf.

Because the photos were not taken in a standard black and white studio style, they have prompted various discussions over the years as to when and where they were taken and for what purpose. Later they would appear on the cover of several magazines, but it remains a mystery as to whether or not they were taken as part of the Columbia contract. This does seem the most likely scenario, however, especially when we note that Miehle does not appear to have worked with Marilyn after that.

While the Twentieth Century Fox contract mainly revolved around a series of publicity appearances and not much else, Columbia's seemed to be more positive. Marilyn was cast in *Ladies of the Chorus*, which started production on 22 April 1948 and ended on 3 May 1948, giving her the opportunity of acting for the first time in a leading role. The film itself may have been considered a B-movie, but Marilyn was so excited she immediately telephoned columnist Louella Parsons to tell her the news.

Gushing about the contract, the young actress told Parsons that she felt her support was responsible for helping the actress to win the role. The journalist had previously given Marilyn some rather favourable mentions in her column and was happy to hear about the

Opposite: Marilyn is looking demure but radiant in this publicity shot. (From the collection of Dionne Abraham)

part, but she assured the starlet that it was her own beauty and talent that had won the role. After the call, Parsons took the opportunity of mentioning Marilyn and the call in her column, describing her as 'such a pretty girl'.

Marilyn put everything she had into making sure she was prepared for her part in *Ladies of the Chorus* and worked with drama coach Natasha Lytess to learn her lines. In the hour-long film, she plays a burlesque dancer who works with her mother (Adele Jergens) in a chorus line. The storyline meant that not only was Marilyn able to show off her acting skills but, in the numbers *Every Baby Needs a Da Da Daddy* and *Anyone Can See I Love You*, her dance and singing styles too. She was also able to act as a love interest to Randy Carroll (played by Rand Brooks) and show a variety of different emotions on screen.

After shooting, Marilyn was under the impression that her performance had been top-notch and that she would soon be cast in an important Columbia movie. The studio continued to send out publicity photos to the press, including some of her practising yoga, one modelling a new metallic swimsuit and another wearing a smart suit. She was also taken to the Town House Hotel on Wilshire Boulevard, where she posed in another set of swimsuit shots, this time leaning on the diving board and pool steps. After that, the un-named photographer took her to the tennis court of the hotel, where she was snapped once again.

Everything looked positive, until one day in September 1948 when she was called to a meeting with one of the Columbia studio executives. 'I was happy as I entered the office,' she said, 'and waited patiently until the man in charge spoke. He looked at me for a long moment and then said, "Miss Monroe we believe in you, and think you'll go far. But at the moment we have nothing for you at this studio." Then he added that my option had been dropped, and the meeting came to a sudden end … Everything crashed in a heap.'

'Miss Monroe we believe in you, and think you'll go far'

The Columbia contract was not a success, but *Ladies of the Chorus* did give Marilyn a great deal of experience and some much-needed confidence to head further down the acting path. It also gave her a

career first when her name appeared on a cinema billboard, advertising the movie. 'I kept driving past the theatre with my name on the marquee,' she said. 'Was I excited! I wished they were using Norma Jeane though, so that all the kids at the home and schools who never noticed me could see it.'

While the film itself did not win any awards, some critics were kind to the story and especially to the 'talented blonde newcomer Marilyn Monroe', as *Medicine Hat Daily News* described her. They also said it was a 'sparkling backstage story of the burlesque world'. *The Showmen's Trade Review* was less kind, however, and declared *Ladies of the Chorus* to have 'entertaining musical numbers to compensate for poor performances and a trite story'. Marilyn, the reviewer said, 'shows promise of bigger things in her rendition of vocal numbers, but her acting will have to improve'.

At the very moment she was dropped from Columbia, Marilyn was taking part in a play called *Stage Door*, which ran at the Bliss-Hayden Theatre from 15 August to 12 September 1948. Still, the play may have given her experience but it did not pay for rent or drama lessons, so in that regard she went back to posing for pin-ups. 'Modelling was a hard grind,' she said, 'even when I got the jobs. My lessons took every cent I could make. Some days I didn't eat so much … At the same time I started doing some serious thinking. You're not fired twice without good reason I thought, and if all this kept up, it could get to be a demoralizing habit … I studied very hard whenever I had free time during the day and in the evenings. My social life, as a result, became practically non-existent, but I felt that the progress I was making was worth it.'

During the next phase of her modelling career, many swimsuit pictures of Marilyn were taken and appeared in a variety of magazines and newspapers. In October 1948 her picture was used to demonstrate good posture, while in November she provided photographs to go with an article on adopting a healthy skin-care routine. In the pictures the model was seen applying lipstick, while the caption declared

'I wished they were using Norma Jeane, so that all the kids at the home and schools who never noticed me could see it'

Opposite: Marilyn visited the Town House hotel in order to have a variety of publicity photos taken using locations such as the tennis courts and pool. (Top photo from the collection of Michelle Morgan, bottom photo from the collection of Dionne Abraham)

she was a 'pretty girl [with] pretty lips'. Her photos were also used in a 1949 article to advise on the benefits of swimming and keeping fit: 'A daily swim, indoors or out, helps starlet Marilyn Monroe keep her figure trimmed for the camera's revealing lens.'

'A daily swim, indoors or out, helps starlet Marilyn Monroe keep her figure trimmed for the camera's revealing lens'

May 1949 saw her return to the Pan Pacific Auditorium, where the Pacific Coast Antiques Show was taking place. There, wearing shorts and a sweater, the actress was photographed sitting on vintage furniture that was to be on display during the show. 'Marilyn Monroe takes years off a Victorian miniature chair,' the *Los Angeles Times* told their readers. Before the day was over, she posed alongside another tiny chair, as well as a bowling ball. Then Marilyn managed to look extremely at ease riding a huge penny-farthing bicycle. Miss Snively later mentioned the latter photograph in her list of Blue Book photographs, and since she had connections at the Pan Pacific, it is very possible that this job came as a result of the actress's still occasional association with the agency. From the confidence shown by the model that day it is also clear that she had come a long way since the Holga Steel photos of 1945, and Miss Snively most certainly played a big hand in that positive development.

While the Antiques Show photographs did not raise the slightest hint of an eyebrow, others that she posed for in 1949 were to come back to haunt her later in her career. Probably the toughest year in terms of money, 1949 saw the model/actress have a variety of cash-flow problems, and there were times when she wondered which way to turn. One day, a man called to offer money and other luxuries in exchange for certain favours:

Opposite: A publicity head shot from around 1948. (From the archive of Ben and Astrid Franse)

For a dizzy moment I had visions of being able to pay my rent but as he went on giving the details of what I would be expected to do, my visions vanished. He was brutally frank and all I could think of to say was that he shouldn't talk that way over a public telephone. I didn't realise how silly that sounded until I hung up and then I started to laugh.

At the time of the call, she was late with her rent at the Hollywood Studio Club and threatened with eviction. Marilyn knew she did not wish to have anything to do with the perverse caller, but, still, something had to be done about her situation. She picked up the telephone and called Tom Kelley, who had used her in the past for a beer advert. He had asked her several times to pose nude and she always refused, but this time it was her home on the line and she felt she may not have much choice. However, if the session was going to go ahead, Marilyn did have a particular requirement – she would only take her clothes off for him if accompanied by his wife, Natalie.

One model who worked for Kelley at the time remembers Natalie as a stern woman who seemed rather jealous of the scantily clad women who frequented his studio. The two women did not get along, and one day the model was suddenly dropped and told she would never work for the photographer again. The reason given was that Kelley did not want to work with women who had children, but the model – who had posed for him as a mother since the beginning of their

working relationship – always believed this to be untrue. Instead, she blamed her tense relationship with Natalie as the real reason she was asked to leave.

Marilyn, however, did not seem to have any problems at all in that direction, and in May 1949 she posed nude for the photographer while lying on a blanket of red velvet. 'I decided I'd be safer with [Kelley] than with some rich old guy who might catch me in a weak moment when I was hungry and didn't have enough to buy a square meal,' Marilyn explained. 'Kelley told me he'd camouflage my face, but it turned out everybody recognized me.' When later asked what it felt like to be photographed in such a way, she wittily answered, 'It was drafty,' and added that the only thing she had on that day was the radio. 'When I see the

Above and opposite: Two gorgeous publicity head shots. Marilyn gave these to her friend, Bill Pursel (From the collection of Bill Pursel)

photos now,' she said years later, 'I feel like I'm dressing in a room without window shades.'

Kelley later told biographer Maurice Zolotow that he paid Marilyn $50 for her services and then sold the rights to a calendar maker for $500. 'He made a fortune on it,' Kelley said. 'Sold close to 8,000,000 calendars.' The calendar maker, John Baumgarth, spoke about the deal himself: 'I'd only printed a few of these calendars and had even forgotten the girl's name when one day my secretary shoved the calendar under my nose and said, "Know who this is? It's Marilyn Monroe." "You're crazy" I answered, but it was.' The nude photographs would eventually hit the headlines in 1952, but instead of destroying her career, as the studio thought it would, the scandal actually won the actress much sympathy after she announced that the reason she had posed in the first

'I feel like I'm dressing in a room without window shades'

place was because without the money she would have been evicted from her apartment. Fans appreciated her candour and Marilyn's fame continued to rise.

Back in the 1940s, her film career limped on until she was offered a part in the Marx Brothers movie *Love Happy*, playing a client of Grunion (played by Groucho Marx). This small but significant role made sure her career turned a corner, and she found herself off on a big promotional tour in support of the movie. The trip took in Detroit, Chicago and New York, where they happened to be in the middle of a heat wave. Marilyn, however, arrived in a woollen suit:

> I had never been to New York; I thought it was always cold there, so I came in all wool – in the middle of summer! It was so hot that I spent all the rest of my visit in a cotton dress. I bought a beret since I'd heard that in the east people wore hats. It was my first trip east and my first hat.

During the trip, Marilyn made various publicity appearances, including the opening of a *Photoplay Dream House*, which required her to travel to Warrensburg on 21 June 1949. While there, she took part in a radio broadcast and posed with the various high-tech items in the home. She also did her first interview with celebrated columnist Earl Wilson, and although he would later become a staunch supporter and friend of the actress, at this particular time he seemed to have no interest in her at all. Together they talked about her nickname of the Mmmm Girl, and the reporter asked what she thought of the tag given to her. 'I'm sure none of the girls ever got hurt by being called such names,' she told Wilson, who remained – for now – totally unimpressed by her star quality.

Opposite: Love Happy *gave Marilyn the opportunity of touring the country on a publicity trip. It also gave her some beautiful head shots, such as this one. (From the collection of Livia Vidicki)*

Below: This press photo was taken during the Love Happy *tour. Note how the publication has whitened the background in preparation for the photo being placed into an article. Unknown photographer. (From the collection of Livia Vidicki)*

Away from the press calls and publicity appearances, Marilyn took some time off from her schedule to pose once again for Andre De Dienes, this time on a beach, playing with a large, polka-dot umbrella. Another photographer captured her poolside whilst wearing several different swimsuits. The latter pictures are some of the prettiest taken during this period, but the circumstances surrounding their creation remains something of a mystery. Over the years it has been reported that the man who took the shots was Arthur Weegee, who later became famous for distorting black and white shots of various celebrities, including Marilyn herself. However, after some investigation, including talking to the Weegee estate, it still cannot be established for sure if he was the photographer or not.

Further confusion comes on the location of the session. It certainly seems to have taken place on the East Coast, and some believe it to have been at Jones Beach pool in Long Island. A newspaper article published in May 1953 seems to suggest otherwise. In the piece, columnist Earl Wilson explains that several years before Marilyn became famous she posed for poolside pictures in the Bronx. However, in

Marilyn posing on a diving board at a New York pool. Unknown photographer. (From the collection of Kim Goodwin)

some of the shots, her pink costume was considered too 'flesh-coloured' and the *New York Daily News* refused to print it. This article certainly seems to be referring to one of the colour shots from the session, but it does not mention a photographer.

Another article, this time from 1949, is no more informative. It shows Marilyn modelling a different swimsuit but seemingly from the same session, and it includes a rather questionable caption, describing her as emerging out of the pool and almost out of her suit. Because no trace can be found of the photographs or negatives in the Weegee archive, it would seem that it shall forever remain a mystery as to whether or not the famed photographer took the beautiful shots.

After the success of the publicity tour, Marilyn continued her ambitions to finally hit the big time. 'There were some difficult days and some pleasant ones,' she recalled. 'I went to school, held down a number of jobs, looked for opening in pictures all the time, had many disappointments which were very crushing and finally reached some small measure of success.' These new accomplishments had rather a lot to do with her acting agent, Johnny Hyde, who was determined to push her career forward and make sure doors opened up for Marilyn. Through all her hard work, she was cast in a variety of parts, including a small role in *A Ticket to Tomahawk*, which called upon her dance and singing skills for several scenes. The experience wasn't an altogether positive one, however, as, during location shooting in Colorado, Marilyn became extremely ill and was sick for most of her scenes. Columnist

Marilyn at a New York pool. Unknown photographer. (From the collection of Kim Goodwin)

Marilyn poses in her bikini at a New York pool. (From the collection of Kim Goodwin)

Opposite: Marilyn publicity photo. (From the collection of Michelle Morgan)

Jimmie Fidler told readers that the illness was the result of a reaction to the high altitudes, and that as far as the actress was concerned, the film should be re-titled *The Girl with the Green Face* instead of *A Ticket to Tomahawk.*

Her biggest break came in *The Asphalt Jungle,* and the first person to hear the news of her casting was old friend and supporter Louella Parsons. Marilyn phoned the columnist and told her all about 'the biggest part of my life', declaring that she was grateful to agent Johnny Hyde, director John Huston and executive and friend Joseph Schenck. 'I am grateful to everyone,' she gushed to the newspaper columnist, who wrote all about it in an October 1949 column. Ultimately, the success of these small but important roles would win Marilyn another contract with Twentieth Century Fox and lead her closer and closer to Hollywood stardom. Sadly, it also led her further and further away from the Blue Book Agency and, of course, Miss Snively.

In the archive, the agency boss does not go into any detail about what it was like when Marilyn finally told her she was leaving modelling for good. Perhaps this was because there was never any official 'goodbye' talk. The model had been going back and forth to the agency for the past five years, though her appearances there were becoming more and more irregular. It is easy to imagine that Miss Snively most likely thought she would be back again when things got tough. Sadly for her, however, this time Marilyn really was headed to pastures new, and it would take her a long time to get back in touch.

SEVEN

THERE'S NO BUSINESS LIKE SHOW BUSINESS

Once Marilyn had put her modelling days behind her, Miss Snively was left saddened. She had known for a long time that the young woman was on her way to great stardom; indeed, she had often pushed her towards this, putting her in touch with people like Helen Ainsworth, who would help fulfil her dreams. However, her disappearance from the agency office left a large hole, and Miss Snively would spend the next twenty years desperately searching for another girl to take her place.

At first Marilyn stayed in touch with the agency sporadically, but eventually her calls dried up when she became too busy. This is detailed in the agency files:

Having always been a hard worker, the new Marilyn Monroe studied with all the gusto she had put into her modelling career, and just as with the magazine covers, the movies to her credit began to grow. Her calls to Miss Snively became less and less frequent. When Marilyn appeared on the cover of *Life*, Miss Snively wrote her a letter congratulating her. No answer.

The magazine mentioned in her notes was the 7 April 1952 edition of *Life*, featuring a photograph of Marilyn by celebrated photographer Philippe Halsman. Wearing a white, off-the-shoulder dress, Marilyn posed with her hair short and eyes half-closed. Halsman had photographed her before – during 1949 for another *Life*

New York business card to Miss Snively's secretary, Joyce Ryan. (From the archive of Ben and Astrid Franse)

photo spread. The young actress had acted out a variety of acting situations for him, and he was so impressed that he told her she should move to New York and pursue an acting career. Marilyn was grateful for his encouragement, but moving to the East Coast was not in her plans at that time.

By the early 1950s, one person who was interested in moving there was Miss Snively herself. 'Most of the magazines were located in New York,' she wrote. 'So [I] moved the headquarters to be closer to the action.' She still maintained an office in Los Angeles, though her association with the actress was all but lost. 'Several years slipped by and Marilyn and Miss Snively were out of contact,' the notes say. 'Marilyn's star shined brilliantly and each went their own ways.'

It was during Miss Snively's time in New York that a young woman by the name of Jayne Mansfield walked into the West Coast office. Jayne was a huge Marilyn fan and so it probably shouldn't come as much of a surprise to discover that she rather liked the idea of joining her old agency. Miss Snively's colleague Maria Smith took one look at the blonde and knew her boss would be interested. Meanwhile, Miss Snively was quickly realising that not much was different in New York after all, and the only real time the agency hit the headlines was when one of their girls was involved in a car accident and threatened to sue the person responsible. Aside from that, there wasn't much in New York that couldn't be done at home, so she packed up the agency files and headed back west.

Opposite: A confident, sleek-looking Marilyn posing for a publicity photo. (From the collection of Dionne Abraham)

Above: Jayne Mansfield and her husband, Mickey Hargitay, greet Miss Snively. Mansfield always held her former boss in high regard. Unknown photographer. (From the archive of Ben and Astrid Franse)

Opposite: As a model, Mansfield posed with fellow starlets, just as Marilyn had done before her. Unknown photographer. (From the archive of Ben and Astrid Franse)

Once there, Miss Snively was introduced to Jayne Mansfield and liked what she saw. The model was signed to the agency and sent to see photographers immediately. 'She wasn't with me too long,' Miss Snively later said. 'Because she was moving fast. She stepped into pictures the next year. Now she's a Broadway star and signed to a new long-term Fox contract.'

'Marilyn's career was on the up, but it came at a price'

The two women became friends and kept in touch even after the model had left Blue Book. In the agency archive there are several photographs of the blonde bombshell: one with Miss Snively herself and one showing Jayne with other models. However, there is also another, more personal, photograph of the actress, this time showing off her newborn baby, Miklos, just days before Christmas 1958. On the back of the photograph the actress has written a loving note, telling Miss Snively that her baby weighed almost 10lb and was born healthy. She also tells her friend and former boss that in order to give thanks for the safe arrival, both she and her husband would be donating money to the Children's Asthma and Research Institute, and then encourages her to do the same.

Miss Snively made many notes and lists about the photographers her models worked with. (From the archive of Ben and Astrid Franse)

While Miss Snively continued with business matters, Marilyn's career was on the up, but it came at a price. Whereas photographers had always built her up during her modelling career, now it seemed that critics and detractors were just as eager to knock her down. She became lonely and in 1952 told reporter Sid Ross that the publicity she was receiving was making her rather shy and afraid. 'I'm beginning to feel like a piece of statuary that people are inspecting with a magnifying glass,' she said. '[They are] looking for imperfections – taking apart my dress, my voice, my figure, my acting – everything about me.'

Meanwhile, Miss Snively was still eager to publicise her business with photographs of Marilyn, either in articles, literature or the Blue Book catalogue itself. She wrote down copious amounts of notes about the photos Marilyn had posed in and kept lists of the photographers and descriptions of their work. She also began writing to various magazines, offering her photos and expert information for their articles. On 28 November 1953 she sent a letter to Gordon Manning, Managing Editor at *Colliers* magazine, and copied in *Life* and the *Saturday Evening Post*:

Dear Mr Manning

Enclosed please find three photographs of Norma Jeane Dougherty, now known as Marilyn Monroe. I have what is probably considered the most complete file on this girl, dating back to 1945, when she did her first modelling job under my direction.

This file consists of approximately sixty photographs made by fifteen amateur and professional photographers from the start of her career in 1945, up to and including her first $75.00 a week contract at Twentieth Century Fox. These pictures with full and complete captions and story are being offered for sale to you at this time. I would appreciate your early consideration of this matter.

Very truly yours

Emmeline Snively.

Similar letters were sent to other publications including *Pageant*, who turned down the offer, just as *The Saturday Evening Post* did too, but *People Today* published an article entitled 'I taught Marilyn how' in their April 1954 issue. In return, Miss Snively received a hefty sum of $150 for her services, and she wrote to the magazine to share her feelings on 3 April: 'I want to thank you for sticking exactly to the truth on my story of Marilyn Monroe,' she wrote. 'So many stories on her have been twisted around to make them have more sensational news value.'

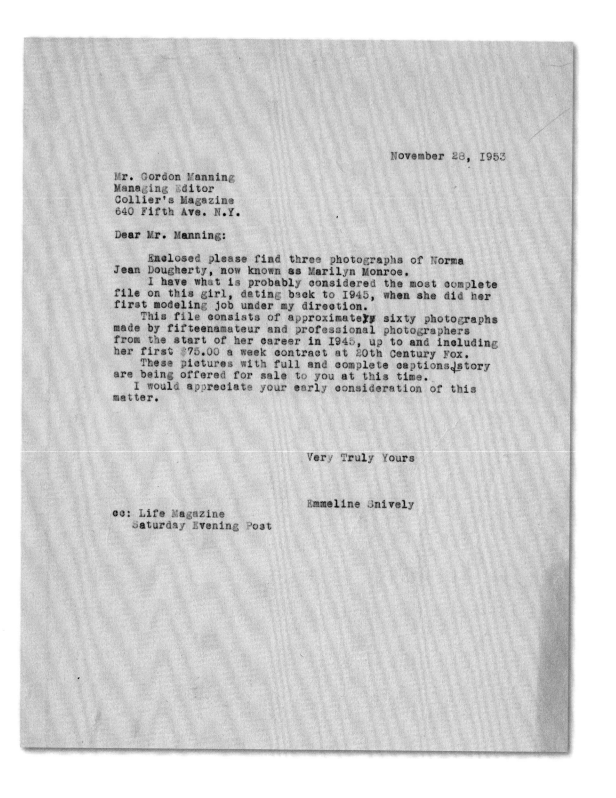

November 28, 1953

Mr. Gordon Manning
Managing Editor
Collier's Magazine
640 Fifth Ave. N.Y.

Dear Mr. Manning:

Enclosed please find three photographs of Norma
Jean Dougherty, now known as Marilyn Monroe.
I have what is probably considered the most complete
file on this girl, dating back to 1945, when she did her
first modeling job under my direction.
This file consists of approximately sixty photographs
made by fifteen amateur and professional photographers
from the start of her career in 1945, up to and including
her first $75.00 a week contract at 20th Century Fox.
These pictures with full and complete captions, story
are being offered for sale to you at this time.
I would appreciate your early consideration of this
matter.

                              Very Truly Yours

                              Emmeline Snively

cc: Life Magazine
    Saturday Evening Post

April 3, 1954

Mr. Vincent T. Tajiri,
Art Photography
Chicago, Illinois

Dear Mr. Tajiri,

At long last I have assembled a collection of photographs of
Marilyn Monroe that I believe will be of interest to your readers.
I am receiving a great many bids for this material ,and would like
to agree on price before I send the set along.

How many prints are you interested in.?They are photos of
Marilyn in various costumes and poses , shot by eight or ten
different photographers, also, I have some color transparencies.
Karl Leaf, who suggested that I show you this material in
the first place, plans to be in Chicago about the time this letter
arrives there, and plans to see you.

I will appreciate hearing from you, and if all is agreeable
will send the photos post haste.

Very sincerely yours,

Emmeline Snively

*Opposite: Letter from
Miss Snively to Colliers
magazine. (From the
archive of Ben and Astrid
Franse)*

*Letters from Miss Snively
to Art Photography
magazine. (From the
archive of Ben and Astrid
Franse)*

April 24, 1954

Mr. Vincent T. Tajiri,
Art Photography
Chicago, Ill.

Dear Mr. Tajiri:

Believe it or not, The Marilyn Monroe Materialis on it's
way.I selected 16 photos., one magazine cover composite,
and ome picture of me for you to choose from. I believe
they tell the story. Willinger and Bienes didnt contribute
any in the last analysis. Included are two shots that have
been published , one 4 by 5 numbered A by David Conover,
Marilyn's first picture, and no. 16 by the late John
Randolph.(This has a note of explanation)

The contributing photographers all have releases,
and know that I am selling them., however I would like
to give each man credit. Also I have some color transparencies should you be interested.They are by Miller,
Randolph, and Jasgur.

I make no claim to fame as a typist or writer,
as you already know, so please feel free to reorganize
my material to suit your needs. Each photograph is
captioned, and I have tried to present them in chronological
order.

Thank you for your patience. I would appreciate
it if you would return the prints to me when you have
finished with them.

Very truly yours,

Emmeline Snively

Page 1

How I developed Marilyn Monroe from a rookie model to her first screen

test at Fox Studios.

The head of a famous school tells what it takes to go from

model training to pictures.

Sketch signed by E. S.

After twelve years of running a model school and agency in Hollywood

I've worked with lots of girls and "developed" some of the successful

names in movies and fashion, but the biggest and one of the most

satisfying discoveries was the finding of a raw little cornfed,

would-be model named Norma Jean Dougherty and grooming her into the

first film test -- from which she blossomed into the lustrous star now

known as Marilyn Monroe.

How it happened is in a way a typical story. Not so much one of

the immediate jumps that film aspirants dream of, as the real life

job filled with ups and downs -- plenty of hard work and determination

on Norma Jean's part and good solid work on my part to analyze and

develop her best points (no pun intended) to where they would be

recognized.

People are apt to think the glamorous star they see was always that

way or just as glamorous. Or that she was a poorly dressed beauty that

changed overnite from moth to butterfly. Actually such careers are

just as much a process of change and struggle as in nine out of

ten other careers.

When I met Norma Jean Dougherty in 1945 she was just 18 (describe

appearance and circumstances) working as _____.

Even then she always had an eager smile. I was running as I am now

the Blue Book Model Agency and had a model school where I took girls

I felt had _____and taught them, just as the

Miss Snively's article notes.
(From the archive of Ben
and Astrid Franse)

John R. Powers School does in New York. I also acted as agent for   Page 2

girls from my school and free-lance models and actresses who wanted

to work in movies and fashion shows.

Hollywood, being the kind of spot it is, there were hundreds of

girls that wanted and needed this kind of help. They came from all

over the country or grew up right there.

At the time Norma Jean walked in I had 30 girls in school. I was

doing fashion shows, promoting photographic models for fashion-

illustration and cover work, as well as publicity assignments for the

Orange Show. I had handled many girls who ultimately made the grade

in motion pictures including Mala Powers, so I knew my business.

I signed her up -- analyzed her -- she had figure, clothes were

wrong and didn't do justice to her figure. Her hair was wrong --

careless mass and too curly -- didn't bring out her features. She

no make-up at all but had good skin, eyes and teeth. For the

year I did a lot of changing and thinking on Norma Jean

...rty or Marilyn Monroe to you.

...did this......

...got her a job. She was scared to death. When the photographs

came in we studied them, asked the photographer for tips and hints

in order to help her and groom her _fast!_ She was open to suggestion

and criticism -- ate it up in fact. Was more than eager to please.

Voice   --   deep breath   --   liked people.

Then came period of depression -- accident -- conscientious --

reliable. I got her work ...

She earned $5.00 per hour -- artists and calendars -- sketching,

Earl Moran. She bleached hair for ad -- popularity affected.

Acceptance by photographers and illustrators.

Wasn't interested in movies.

Married and couldn't enter contests.

Attitude toward other cover girls in agency and school.

All along we'd been planning -- She didn't want to test.

An article also appeared in *Modern Screen* in July 1954, *Art Photography* in October, and other magazines and newspapers after that. *Life* magazine was eager to hear more about Miss Snively's collection but in the end decided that the photos were not suited to their immediate needs. However, all the attention her articles did receive threatened to saturate the market. The editor of *Art Photography* wrote to say that it was 'unfortunate' that *Modern Screen* was using much of the same material as they were planning to but hoped that it wouldn't conflict with their story. Still, the thought of duplication did not seem to worry Miss Snively too much, and she continued to talk about Marilyn in the years ahead, both in print, television and film.

One article was typed out by Miss Snively and filed away in the archive, complete with notes to herself, prompts, random words and blank spaces:

How I developed Marilyn Monroe from a rookie model to her first screen test at Fox Studios. The head of a famous school tells what it takes to go from model training to pictures.

Sketch signed by E.S.

After twelve years of running a model school and agency in Hollywood I've worked with lots of girls and 'developed' some of the successful names in movies and fashion, but the biggest and one of the most satisfying discoveries was the finding of a raw little corn fed airplane worker and would-be model named Norma Jeane Dougherty and grooming her into the first film test – from which she blossomed into the lustrous star now known as Marilyn Monroe.

How it happened is in a way a typical story. Not so much one of the immediate jumps that film aspirants dream of, as the real life job [was] filled with ups and downs – plenty of hard work and determination on Norma Jeane's part and good solid work on my part to analyse and develop her best points (no pun intended) to where they would be recognised.

People are apt to think the glamorous star they see was always that way or just as glamorous. Or that she was a poorly dressed beauty that changed overnight from moth to butterfly. Actually such careers are just as much a process of change and struggle as in nine out of ten other careers.

When I met Norma Jeane Dougherty in 1945 she was just eighteen (describe appearance and circumstances) working as _____. Even then she always had an eager smile. I was running as I am now the Blue Book Model Agency and had a model school where I took girls I felt had _____ and taught them just as the John R Powers school does in New York. I also acted as agent for girls from my school and freelance models and actresses who wanted to work in movies and fashion shows.

Hollywood, being the kind of spot it is, there were hundreds of girls that wanted and needed this kind of help. They came from all over the country or grew up right there.

At the time Norma Jeane walked in, I had thirty girls in school. I was doing fashion shows, promoting photographic models for fashion illustration and cover work, as well as publicity assignments for the Orange Show. I had handled many girls who ultimately made the grade in motion pictures, including Mala Powers, so I knew my business.

I signed her up – analysed her – she had figure, clothes were all wrong and didn't do justice to her figure. Her hair was wrong – shapeless mass and too curly – didn't bring out her features. She wore no make-up at all but had good skin, eyes and teeth. For the next year I did a lot of changing and thinking on Norma Jeane Dougherty, or Marilyn Monroe to you.

We did this …

And got her a job. She was scared to death. When the photographs came in we studied them, asked the photographer for tips and hints to help and groom her fast. She was open to suggestion and criticism – ate it up in fact. Was more than eager to please.

Voice – deep breath – liked people.

Then came a period of depression – accident – conscientious – reliable. I got her work …

She earned $5.00 per hour – artists and calendars – sketching, Earl Moran. She bleached hair for ad – popularity affected.

Acceptance by photographers and illustrators.

Wasn't interested in movies.

Married and couldn't enter contests.

Attitude toward other cover girls in agency and school.

All along we'd been planning – She didn't want to test.

The John R. Powers mentioned in Miss Snively's notes was the founder of a model school and agency in New York, which taught perspective starlets to make the most of themselves and break into the business. Powers was often quoted in the newspapers as saying that he believed any woman could be attractive given the right skills. This philosophy made him one of the most popular and powerful of all the agency directors, and it is easy to see why Miss Snively was greatly inspired by his work.

Interestingly, while she strived to be just like him, the two agencies were actually already alike in many ways, and both saw at least several women move from modelling into acting over the years. Of course, no model was ever more successful at that than Marilyn, and in 1946 it would seem that Powers actually wanted her to go out to New York and sign with his agency. She said no in favour of concentrating on modelling and acting in Los Angeles, which meant that, at that moment at least, Miss Snively had eclipsed the very agency she was trying to live up to.

As 1954 progressed, the Blue Book director was happy to discover that Marilyn was currently making *There's No Business Like Show Business* at Twentieth Century Fox. Miss Snively decided to contact her old client again, as notes in the archive reveal:

She called the studio to see if Marilyn would pose for some publicity pictures for Blue Book Models. Marilyn quickly agreed and was excited about seeing Miss Snively. Miss Snively showed up [at the studio] with a cap and gown but Marilyn's hair was in curlers, so the pictures were made of Marilyn's measurements being taken by Miss Snively. She had brought along a picture to be autographed but Marilyn had just had new publicity pictures made and insisted that Miss Snively have one of those. This was the favourite picture she was to have.

The pictures taken on the set that day show Marilyn in the costume she wore to perform a song and dance number called *Heat Wave*. The actress wasn't a huge fan of the song, and her new husband, baseball star Joe DiMaggio, wasn't an admirer of the outfit, considering it too revealing for his wife to wear. However, neither seemed to bother Miss Snively, and photos show there is no doubt that Marilyn enjoyed meeting up with her old mentor once again.

'there is no doubt that Marilyn enjoyed meeting up with her old mentor once again'

Her joy is there for all to see, as the agency boss measures her hips and bust, while comparing the statistics to those in her famous Blue Book. Miss Snively did not send her bust measurement photographs out for publication, thinking it too risqué. The hips photograph was considered a much safer option, and that quickly became the better known of the two shots.

The visit to the set wasn't all happiness it would seem, as Miss Snively later recalled having a private word with Marilyn off set. During the quiet talk, the actress confessed that she felt inadequate in her career:

> She didn't really feel she was a qualified actress, [but] how could she have felt any different? She'd signed her first contract before she had her first acting lesson. God I wanted to cry for her then. This can be the loneliest town in the world and it's even lonelier for you if you're on top of the heap.

Incidentally, another old friend she encountered during this time was artist and photographer Earl Moran. While it is not known if he visited on the same day as Miss Snively, he later recalled that Marilyn hugged him on the set and thanked him for making her legs look wonderful in the portraits he did of her. Moran later explained that the actress thought her ankles were too thin and loved what he did to make them look good.

Once contact between Miss Snively and Marilyn had been established again, the actress suddenly began phoning her old mentor. It does not seem to have been on a regular basis, but it was certainly

Opposite: Marilyn signed and presented this publicity photo to Miss Snively, when they were reunited on the set of There's No Business Like Show Business. *(From the archive of Ben and Astrid Franse)*

enough to give the agency boss hope that she had not been forgotten during her protégé's rise to the top. Several months after the meeting on *There's No Business Like Show Business*, she decided once again that it would be nice to use a photo of the star in Blue Book Agency literature. She wrote to Sonya Wolfson in the Twentieth Century Fox publicity department to ask for permission:

> Dear Miss Wolfson,
>
> You were kind enough to arrange an interview and picture session for me with Marilyn Monroe last fall, during the shooting of 'No Business Like Show Business.' – Enclosed find 4 x 5 shot of same.
>
> You may remember Marilyn graduated from my school – Blue Book Models – and did her photographic modelling through my agency.
>
> I would like permission to use her photograph in my Model School Brochure and classified telephone book advertisement. I would use either a recent picture or one of my early ones …

It is not known if Twentieth Century Fox ever replied to Miss Snively, but certainly the archives are full of letters and documents from around this time, all trying to interest various branches of the media in the association between Marilyn and Blue Book. In July 1955 *Redbook* magazine published a beautiful photograph of the actress on their cover that caught Miss Snively's attention. Seeing an opportunity, she put pen to paper and wrote to the magazine on 18 August 1955:

1169 No. Vine Street, Hollywood 28, Calif.

August 18, 1955

Dear Sir:

Your Lovely July Cover of Marilyn Monroe takes me back to July 1947. One of my photographic model students, Jean Brown, was the first Western girl ever to appear as a RED BOOK COVER GIRL. New York Photographer Runnie Green shot her while he was here on location. Later we received a wire for Richard Miller to use her again, and the resulting station wagon shot was used the next month on the August Cover.

Enclosed please find photos of two students of the BLUE BOOK School of Photographic Modeling, graduates of the same class 1947. On the left Jean Brown....... On the Right, Norma Jean Dougherty. Oh Yes, Norma Jean is now known as Marilyn Monroe........

EMMELINE SNIVELY

DIRECTOR
Blue Book School of Modeling
Hollywood, Calif.

May 18, 1956

Paul Guillumette
475 Fifth Avenue
New York 17, New York

Dear Paul:

I have been meaning to write to you for a long time--wondering if you are keeping up with your photography of Famous Shots and envy- ing your life of travel and no deadline!

Hope you saw my nice paragraph in Time magazine last week, May 14- on Marilyn Monroe. Whenever I am interviewed about her they always pick out the things that were wrong or impossible or problems whe had to overcome. Of course that makes news--but if Marilyn would read what I have been given credit for writing she would have an inferiority complex for sure. She wouldn't even believe I am on her side.

Now here is where you come in! Remember how sold I was on that girl from the very beginning? How I used to write you pages and pages wondering why her color covers didn't sell? I told you how wonderful she was in person and how I wished you could meet her yourself? Then you would write back saying the editors didn't like her unruly hair--that they objected to her smile because it broadened her nose, etc.

I am constantly being interviewed about Marilyn and I need a way to show that I am and always have been more than sold on her

Could I ask a favor of you? Could you write me a letter bringing back those early days--you might say "I saw your nice paragraph in Time magazine on Marilyn Monroe and it brought to my mind the way you had written concerning her covers-etc" as I said above.

I would appreciate this so much Paul--Dick Miller--Andre Dienes-- many of the photographers that you had at the time had material on her and we were some what successful--Eh Wot? Long hand is Okay for the letter and make that signature legible--I want to reprint it.

Love,

Emmeline

Letter from Miss Snively to Redbook *magazine. (From the archive of Ben and Astrid Franse)*

Letter from Miss Snively to Paul Guillumette. (From the archive of Ben and Astrid Franse)

Dear Sir:

Your Lovely July Cover of Marilyn Monroe takes me back to July 1947. One of my photographic model students, Jean Brown, was the first Western girl ever to appear as a RED BOOK COVER GIRL. New York photographer Ruzzie Green shot her while he was here on location. Later we received a wire for Richard Miller to use her again, and the resulting station wagon shot was used the next month on the August cover.

Enclosed please find photos of two students of the BLUE BOOK School of Photographic Modelling, graduates of the same class 1946. On the left Jean Brown ... On the right, Norma Jeane Dougherty. Oh Yes, Norma Jeane is now known as Marilyn Monroe ...

EMMELINE SNIVELY, Director, Blue Book School of Modelling, Hollywood, Calif.

It had now been over ten years since Norma Jeane Dougherty walked into the Blue Book Agency. When Marilyn appeared on the cover of *Time*, on 14 May 1956, Miss Snively was interviewed about her memories of the actress. However, when the article was published, she was not particularly pleased with it and put her thoughts down on paper to an old friend. Miss Snively had known New York photographer Paul Guillumette for many years, as he worked in a photo agency and often tried to place the Blue Book models with East Coast photographers and magazines. She knew that he would remember how hard she pushed for Marilyn's success, and this is obvious in the letter she wrote to him on 18 May 1956:

Dear Paul:

I have been meaning to write to you for a long time – wondering if you are keeping up with your photography of Famous Shots and envying your life of travel and no deadline!

Hope you saw my nice paragraph in *Time* magazine last week, May 14th, on Marilyn Monroe. Whenever I am interviewed about her they always pick out the things that were wrong or impossible or problems she had to overcome. Of course that makes news – but if Marilyn would read what I have been given credit for writing she would have an inferiority complex for sure. She wouldn't even believe I am on her side.

Now here is where you come in! Remember how sold I was on that girl from the very beginning? How I used to write you pages and pages wondering why her colour covers didn't sell? Begging you people to push her? I told you how wonderful she was in person and how I wished you could meet her yourself? Then you would write back saying the editors didn't like her unruly hair – that they objected to her smile because it broadened her nose, etc.

I am constantly being interviewed about Marilyn and I need a way to show that I am and always have been more than <u>sold</u> on her.

Could I ask a favour of you? Could you write me a letter bringing back those early days? You might say 'I saw your nice paragraph in *Time* magazine on Marilyn Monroe and it brought to my mind the way you had written concerning her covers etc.' as I have said above.

I would appreciate this so much Paul. Dick Miller, Andre De Dienes – many of the photographers that you had at the time, had material on her and we were somewhat successful – Eh Wat? Long hand is okay for the letter and make that signature legible – I want to reprint it.

Love
Emmeline.

Several days later, on 21 May 1956, Guillumette wrote a short letter to Miss Snively, saying that he was pleased to read about her in *Time* magazine and that it brought back memories of when they used to correspond about Marilyn. At the very end he wrote that Miss Snively always did her very best to push the young woman, then signed off and posted the letter back to the West Coast.

On the same day Guillumette was writing to her, Miss Snively was working out details of a modelling competition she wished to run to find 'a Marilyn Monroe type, to promote magazine covers, advertising and illustrations'. The proposed press release is located in the archive and reads:

In 1946–1947 [*sic*] BLUE BOOK started Marilyn Monroe. She studied at Blue Book Model's School and became a favourite with photographers as a cover girl and photographic model.

Then Fox signed her—For several years photographers kept calling for the Marilyn Monroe type and Blue Book started several who have since given up modelling for home life.

Then in 1954 we found Jayne Mansfield who seemed to fill the bill – Blue Book sent her to many of Marilyn's former employers – with great success. Earl Moran calendar artist for Brown & Bigelow – Dick Miller cover photographer, Earl Leaf, all thought she had a great future –

Then she donned a red bikini, hit all the columns with her pictures and covers, and made a motion picture or two. All within a year she starred in a New York play and appeared on *Life* magazine in a group of five girls under twenty-five most likely to succeed.

Last week Jayne Mansfield appeared on the cover of *Life* in her own right – having 'arrived' playing (of course) the Marilyn Monroe part in *Will Success Spoil Rock Hunter?* Then lightning struck twice. Fox signed her.

Now BLUE BOOK MODELS is out to find another Marilyn Monroe type.

This literature is interesting and shows Miss Snively's frame of mind at the time. During the years since Marilyn's discovery, she had known her fair share of triumphs and sadness, and her frustration of her two most famous models leaving her is quite clear in the advert. Actor Steve Hayes remembers that at this point she was still a witty, fun lady but had become somewhat cynical and 'short' with people she did not trust. She once told Hayes that

Details of the 'Marilyn Monroe type'. From the archive of Ben and Astrid Franse)

she had been burned too often by people coming into her agency for representation, only to leave her the moment they were offered a bigger and better opportunity elsewhere. Hayes felt that while she still treated her clients very well, there was a part of her that felt she shouldn't treat them too well, just in case they also bolted to another agency.

'her frustration of her two most famous models leaving her is quite clear in the advert'

Nearly a week after typing up her notes related to finding another Marilyn, Miss Snively wrote a much longer proposal of what she wanted to achieve from the competition and what would be expected of the models. She noted that the event was in response to 'popular demand by photographers' and prophesised that it would be called Look Alike, Cinderella Girl or Modern Cinderella. The object of the exercise: 'To look like Marilyn Monroe (gimmick) silver lame dress formerly owned by Marilyn Monroe.' She then urged amateur models to check their credentials. 'How do you look like Marilyn?' she asked, before listing a number of different ways: face, smile, eyes, hair, figure, walk, personality and colouring.

The judges of the competition were to be Norma Jeane-related people: Earl Moran, Earl Leaf, Helen Ainsworth, Richard Miller and Hal Bloom. Directly underneath this, Miss Snively detailed what Blue Book wanted to achieve by doing the competition:

1 – to interview all girls entering contest (could take a Polaroid photo of each)
2 – coupons to bear name and address of Blue Book Model School.
3 – the contest in with current magazine articles and newspaper publicity on Marilyn and Jayne Mansfield.

The prize for the winner would be 'the full Marilyn Monroe treatment – full length courses in the Blue Book School of Modelling Promotion Agency'. This would be accompanied by several other opportunities too, such as posing for Earl Moran, magazine photograph coverage and a picture story with Earl Leaf.

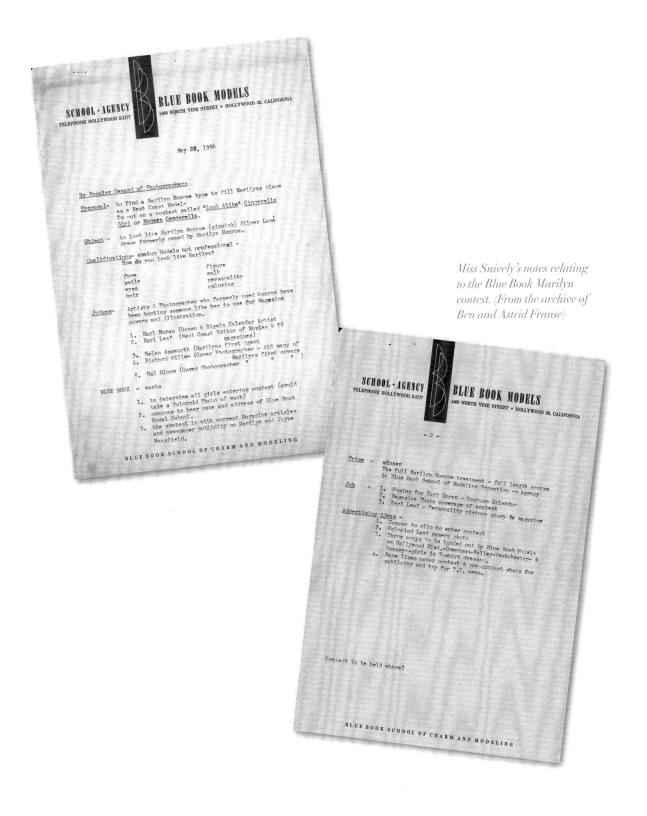

Miss Snively's notes relating to the Blue Book Marilyn contest. (From the archive of Ben and Astrid Franse)

Miss Snively drafted a letter to Marilyn several times before it was ready to send. (From the archive of Ben and Astrid Franse)

5-15-56

D M —

Congratulations — I see you made "time" this week —

It was a most interesting + heart warming story I thought, The Cover is a lovely Portrait + the story should endear you to readers all over the world —

I thank you for sending me Ezra Goodman to see me for my small contribution — You should be proud of the honor as this space is usually reserved for Presidents, Statesmen + Industrialists.

I read somewhere that you always wanted to be on the cover of the Ladies Home Journal. Unfortunately when you were modelling through me those covers were all sent on the East Coast, as were most of the others.

D M

Congratulations! I see you made time this week!

It was a most interesting + heart warming story I thought.

I read somewhere that you always wanted to be on the cover of the Ladies Home Journal — unfortunately when you were modeling all here those covers were with the East Coast

It would mean a great deal to me if I could use your name as a graduate student. In order to be able to do so I need a letter of clearance from you. I have no big advertising plans, but I would appreciate permission. Sometimes I might like to use a little picture as the glamour photo you autographed for me at Fox Studio — (enclosed)

In order to make it easy for you I have enclosed a form

You may be sure that I would use all discretion in this matter + have your greatest interest at heart.

Miss Snively was full of ideas on how she could advertise the contest to make it worthwhile for her and the agency, and wrote down various ways of spreading the word far and wide:

1 – Coupon to clip to enter contest.

2 – Polaroid land camera photo

3 – Throw aways to be handed out by Blue Book Models on Hollywood Boulevard, Downtown, Valley, Westchester and Downey. Girls in T-shirt dresses.

4 – Have *Times* cover content and pre-contest shots for publicity and try for T.V. news.

While Miss Snively was exceptionally keen to make the competition a success, she would first need Marilyn's permission to use her image. She wrote to her around the time she was working on the proposal, and a handwritten version of the letter was later found in the archive. It is translated as follows:

Dear M

Congratulations – I see you made *Time* this week.

It was a most interesting and heart-warming story I thought. The cover is a lovely portrait and the story should endear you to readers all over the world. You should be proud of the honour as this space is usually reserved for Presidents, Statesmen and Industrialists.

I read somewhere that you always wanted to be on the cover of the *Ladies Home Journal.* Unfortunately when you were modelling through me those covers were all situated on the East Coast, as were most of the others.

It would mean a great deal to me if I could use your name as a graduate student. In order to be able to do so I need a letter of clearance from you. I have no big advertising places, but I would appreciate permission.

Sometimes I might like to use a little picture [such] as the glamour photo you autographed for me at Fox Studios (enclosed.) In order to make it easy for you, I have enclosed a form. You may be

sure that I would use all discretion in this matter and have your greatest interest at heart.

While there is no indication as to whether or not Miss Snively received a reply to the letter, it would be safe to say that she probably did not. No details of the reply can be found in the archive, though it would seem that the agency boss did continue with the competition as mention was later made in a local newspaper, complete with a photograph of two lookalike twins.

By the time the letter was sent, the actress was in the midst of shooting *Bus Stop* for Twentieth Century Fox, supporting future husband Arthur Miller through various personal and professional upsets and making plans to travel to London so she could make *The Prince and the Showgirl* with Laurence Olivier. If she had received the letter, it is doubtful that Marilyn would have had the time or inclination at that point to reply to it.

Several years later, on 31 July 1958, Miss Snively wrote to Marilyn again, care of Twentieth Century Fox. Delivered by courier on 2 August, the note was a heartfelt declaration of the agency boss's happiness for what the actress had achieved. The letter Marilyn ultimately received was found in her filing cabinets at the time of her death. An earlier draft was retained by Miss Snively in her own archive. It reads as follows:

Dear Marilyn

Mother and I are so happy to hear that you are back in California making a picture. We have been following your steady progress over the years, and are so proud of your accomplishments.

Our students at BLUE BOOK MODELS regard your constant development and success as an inspiration. I would so like to see you. Would that be possible? I have an idea to discuss with you that I think you will like.

You may reach me at Dunkirk 8-3545 or 617 South Vermont Avenue, Los Angeles 5.

On the copy of the letter, stored carefully for so many years, Miss Snively scribbled the words 'No Answer'.

Opposite: Marilyn talking to a reporter on her return to Hollywood to make Bus Stop *in 1956. Unknown photographer. (From the collection of Ben and Astrid Franse)*

Delivery note for letter sent from Miss Snively to Marilyn in 1958. (From the archive of Ben and Astrid Franse)

Dear Marilyn,

Mother and L are so happy to hear that you are back in California making a picture.
We have been following your steady progress over the years , and are so proud of your accomplishments.
Our students at BLUE BOOK MODELS regard you constant development and success as an insp iration.
I I would so like to see you. Would this be possible?
I have an idea to discuss with you that I think you will like.

You may reach me at DUnkirk 8-3545 or 617 South Vermont Ave, L.A .5,

Letter from Miss Snively to Marilyn with the words 'No answer' scrawled underneath. (From the archive of Ben and Astrid Franse)

While Marilyn (or at least her personal secretary) received and filed the letter away, it is easy to see why the actress did not reply. At the time she was in the midst of a very stressful shoot, making *Some Like It Hot* with Tony Curtis and Jack Lemmon. The trip to Hollywood was the first in two years, since she was now living in New York with her husband Arthur Miller. Her arrival in early July should have been a happy one, but unfortunately she was greeted by a group of very rude newspapermen, who seemed intent on punishing her for leaving California.

One journalist took the rather unsatisfactory decision to ask Marilyn why she had become overweight, which was bizarre, as photos of the event show her to be extremely slim. She smiled sweetly and replied as politely as she could. 'My weight goes up and down like anybody else's but I'll be in good shape in two weeks because I intend to do lots of walking and exercising … I know I have gained a little weight, but I'll work that off rehearsing for the new film.' The next day the *Mirror News* reported on the arrival and returned the verdict that Marilyn was 'chubby'.

During the making of *Some Like It Hot*, Marilyn became pregnant with Miller's child, and she was terrified that the running around she had to do would lead to a miscarriage. The whole experience of making the film was a negative one for all concerned, though thankfully it did go onto become one of the most successful of her career. For Marilyn, however, it had been exceptionally hard work.

After filming had ended, the actress very sadly suffered a miscarriage, just before Christmas 1958. This was to be her second failed attempt at having a child, and the experience was a depressing and heartbreaking one. The letter from Miss Snively was likely forgotten while Marilyn recovered from the loss, so at that point she did not learn why her former boss wanted to contact her. While the final version of the letter was finally released several years ago, the reason for Miss Snively expressing that 'I have an idea to discuss with you' has never been made clear. However, she did reveal what the idea was, shortly after Marilyn's death. 'I thought of getting her interested in working around hospitals where she could come in contact with sick kids who needed someone to love them,' she said. 'I thought maybe that might help. But we

```
                        BLUE BOOK STUDIO OF MODELING

   3757 Wilshire Boulevard              2306 Westwood Boulevard
   Los Angeles 5, California            West Los Angeles, California
   DUnkirk 9-8974                       GRanite 7-4118
   DUnkirk 9-2210

   Your modeling course will cover the following subjects:

   Personal Improvement

        Posture - Grace                 Hands - Feet
        Walking - Pivot                 Sitting - Rising
        Exercise - Balance              Entrance - Exit
        Arms - Head                     Door - Automobile

        Grooming                        Hair Style
        Foundation Garments             Social Graces
        Care of the Body                Putting on Coats
        Skin Care - Make-up             Wardrobe Selection
        Voice and Diction               Line - Color - Fabric

   Fashion Modeling

        Pivot - Routines                Your HAT BOX
        Wholesale Modeling              Fashion Show Make-up
        Retail - Tea Room               Photographic Modeling
        Ramp - Platform                 Your Agency

                        * * * * * * * * * *

   An ADVANCED COURSE of 12 lessons is offered to qualified Models in

   PHOTOGRAPHIC MODELING AND TELEVISION

   This course includes:

        Camera Direction                Costume - Character
        Black and White                 Make-up
        Color - Group Work              Body Control - Action
        Publicity                       Catalogue Fashion
        Advertising                     TV Commercials

                     Professional Presentation

   Under the Personal Supervision of EMMELINE SNIVELY, Director, and
   assisted by top authorities in the fields of:

        PHOTOGRAPHY                     TELEVISION
        FASHION                         MOTION PICTURES
        ADVERTISING

              Our COMPLETE MODEL SERVICE includes
   TRAINING -- AGENCY -- PUBLICITY SERVICE -- CASTING DIRECTORY
```

Modelling course notes. (From the archive of Ben and Astrid Franse)

Opposite: Miss Snively leads a course on television skills. Note the mock TV screen with model sitting behind it. (From the archive of Ben and Astrid Franse)

never got together again any place where we could talk, so it never happened.'

At the same time Marilyn was mourning the loss of her unborn child and trying to move on with her future, Miss Snively was doing everything she could to keep herself and her school in the limelight. She experimented with several different names, including The Central Model Agency and Who's Who, and moved premises several times. Records show that by 1960 her main office was located at 3757 Wilshire Boulevard, while another studio was kept at 2307 Westwood Boulevard. Her modelling courses had adapted to the changing market and now covered additional classes teaching camera direction, TV commercials, catalogue fashion, advertising and motion pictures: 'Our complete model service includes training, agency, publicity service and casting directory,' she wrote in advertising literature:

The Blue Book School of Charm and Modelling offers classes in personal improvement, fashion modelling, photographic modelling, and television commercial training. First impressions are enhanced by correcting posture and weight problems by diet, exercise and rhythm. Make the most of yourself. Stress your good points. Minimize faults and problems. Grooming, wardrobe selection, posture, walking, sitting, make-up, hair care, styling, graceful hands. Favourable lasting impressions are achieved by classes in: etiquette, introductions, tips on interviews, speech.

In the 1960 Blue Book brochure published by the agency, Miss Snively illustrates many of the things that were going on at the time, both in her own career as agency boss and with her clients: 'Miss Snively designed, cast and rehearsed a series of television commercials for an international show account ... She appeared on the Harry Babbit show offering tips on charm and personality development. The models demonstrated.' Photographs of the events show the women exhibiting their skills, under the close supervision of Miss Snively. Another picture shows a second generation model by the name of Lonnie England, who had followed in the footsteps of her mother by signing to the Blue Book Agency.

While they were moving forward into the new decade, some things did not change. There was still a close relationship with Earl Moran, for instance, and when some of the Blue Book girls took part in a hosting event for a glamorous Christmas party, Moran was there with his beautiful wife, Gloria. Showing a photograph of the couple sitting with Miss Snively, text in the advertising literature reads, 'Mr and Mrs Earl Moran enjoyed the punch at the party. Earl is internationally known for his magazine covers and calendars of beauties. Now he is adding photography to his talents. Gloria too paints, specializing in children.'

Opposite: Models go through their paces during one of Miss Snively's Blue Book classes. Unknown photographer. (From the archive of Ben and Astrid Franse)

Package of benefits for the Blue Book agency and school. (From the archive of Ben and Astrid Franse)

Marilyn the Model Calendar notes; 'A Bit About the Contest Director'. (From the archive of Ben and Astrid Franse)

Many famous actresses received their start with Miss Snively. She gave Jayne Mansfield her first job; as a result of the training and promotion at Blue Book Models Marilyn Monroe appeared on countless national magazine covers. Marilyn started with Models Blue Book in 1947.

Miss Emmeline Snively has gained National Recognition for Discovering, Training and Promoting newcomers in the Modeling and Talent Fields.

She received her B.E. degree in Art and Education at U.C.L.A. and continued her graduate work in Art on the Berkeley campus.

A few others who have benefited by the deft touch of Miss Snively are Mala Powers, Motion Picture Star and TV; Jackie O'Donnell, Ed Wynn series, TV; Dwayne Hickman, Bob Cummings show, Loves of Doby Gillis; Ermadine Walters, Song of Bernadette; Frances Ann Rafferty, lead in December Bride, TV; Mary Jane Saunders, Motion Pictures; Elaine Williams, Robert Young Show; Betty Meade, Ken Murray Show; Virginia Hewett, Star of Space Patrol, TV series; Chris Saunders, lead in The Drunkard.

At some point it would seem that the two old friends even planned to put together some kind of Marilyn-related calendar. In the archive there is a sheet of Moran's headed notepaper, on the back of which the couple has scrawled a variety of notes under the heading, 'Marilyn the Model Calendar: List of calendars in colour'. The names of various Earl Moran photos appear on the paper including, 'Bullfighter, Farmerette, Diving, Sailor Girl, Towel and Expression'.

As well as that, they mention Moran's nude photographs, a *Love Happy* publicity picture and the amateur photos from the 1946 Group 13 outing. The name of a New York distributor – Jones Publishing Company – is written towards the bottom of the document, as well as what appears to be a projected price of $1. Whether or not this sheet is solid evidence that the pair were planning a calendar cannot be confirmed. However, it most certainly wouldn't be the last time Miss Snively and Earl Moran planned a Marilyn project together, as shown later in the archive.

While the agency was continuing successfully, Marilyn's life was in turmoil. The year of 1960 was exceptionally tiring, with two movies – *Let's Make Love* and *The Misfits* – taking their toll. A host of personal problems, including a marriage breakdown and various other disasters, was making it a year she was quite keen to forget. Although it had been only fifteen years since the actress had walked into the Blue Book Agency, it could have been a lifetime, and her fabulous modelling days seemed a very long time ago.

'A host of personal problems, including a marriage breakdown and various other disasters, was making it a year she was quite keen to forget'

Back at the agency, Miss Snively remained busy and occasionally became involved as a judge in modelling competitions and other activities. However, her next big project was what she hoped would be a textbook with three possible titles: *How to be a Part-time Model*, *Be a Teen Age Model*, or *Modelling as a Stepping Stone*. She wrote an impassioned letter about the project to a prospective publisher on 13 January 1961:

> Since I have conducted a model school here in Los Angeles for many years, the book could be slanted in several ways. My daily activities result in a life which is a cross between *You Can't Take It With You*, and *My Sister Eileen*, PLUS. The book could be based on my modelling course, telling girls all over the country how to break into the business. I plan to use illustrations [and] photos of course. Would your organization be interested in a book on this subject? Any suggestions appreciated …

As with several of her ideas and aspirations, Miss Snively was unable to get anyone interested in the modelling book, so instead she began to do something totally different: she decided to write a play with secretary Joyce Ryan.

Hidden away for over fifty years, a script entitled *Just Once More, Please* has been found in the Blue Book archive. The document, totalling 132 pages, was written in the early 1960s and was finally finished in 1962. The story revolves around a model agency and the many models and clients that come through its doors. It was, of course,

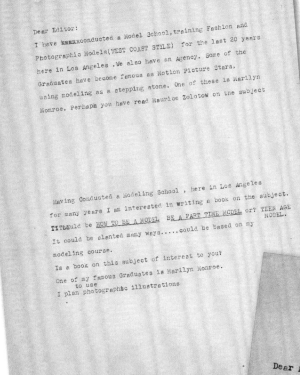

Dear Editor:

I have xxxxxconducted a Model School,training Fashion and
Photographic Models(WEST COAST STYLE) for the last 20 years
here in Los Angeles .We also have an Agency. Some of the
Graduates have become famous as Motion Picture Stars,
using modeling as a stepping stone. One of these is Marilyn
Monroe. Perhaps you have read Maurice Zolotow on the subject

       Having Conducted a Modeling School , here in Los Angeles
for many years I am interested in writing a book on the subject.
TITLEould be HOW TO BE A MODEL BE A PART TIME MODEL or? TEEN AGE
                                                         MODEL.
It could be slanted many ways.....could be based on my
modeling course.
       Is a book on this subject of interest to you?
       One of my famous Graduates is Marilyn Monroe.
            to use
I plan photographic illustrations

Letters to several editors, describing how Miss Snively wishes to write a book about being a model. (From the archive of Ben and Astrid Franse)

                              Jan. 13, 1961
Dear Mr.Muller,
   I am planning to write a book (isn't every-
one?) on the subject of modeling.
   The title might be "How to be a Part Time
Model" .."Be a Teen Age Model"
              "Modeling as a Stepping Stone"to
         T.V. Movies...... etc.
Since I have conducted a Model School here
in Los Angeles for many years the book
could be slanted many ways.
   My daily activities result in a life which
is a cross between "You Cant Take It With
You"   and"My Sister Eileen"PLUS.
The book could be based on my Modeling Course,
telling girls all over the country how to
break in to the business.
   I plan to use illustrations, Photos, of course.
Wouldyour organization be interested in a
book on this subject? Any suggestions
appreciated....

              Sincerely yours,

              Emmeline Snively

based very much on day-to-day life at Blue Book, both past and present. The script describes how the agency looked during the early days when it was known as The Village School:

The curtain rises on the office of the STRIP MODEL AGENCY in Hollywood. 'Strip' refers to the location of the agency, on the Sunset Strip or County Strip, as it is known, between the glamour communities of Hollywood and Beverly Hills.

Originally, the 'ten percenters' (movie and theatrical agents) set up their establishment on these few blocks of county territory to avoid the city taxes. Thus, it has been built up and developed with no building restrictions, a law unto itself, inhabited mostly by antique dealers, body conditioners, night clubs and agents.

The STRIP MODEL AGENCY occupies an old studio-type building that has been converted from time to time with the adding and subtracting of partitions. The decoration relies more on originality and imagination than on money expended. The building is not situated on the street, but with a number of other shops, faces a little drive-in courtyard. It is popularly known as the HUNGARIAN VILLAGE. Two large plate glass windows, almost to the floor are separated by the door and look out on the drive way. Through the left window can be seen the gay entrance of the Bali Café next door where the landlord of the unit holds forth as proprietor of the restaurant.

In the office, thumbtacked to the celotex board on the wall, are numerous photographs of girls, costumed, partially costumed and un-costumed. A bulletin board displays magazine covers, advertising pictures, clippings from newspapers and theatre programs, revealing the talent

Front cover of the script for Miss Snively and Joyce Ryan's play Just Once More, Please. *(From the archive of Ben and Astrid Franse)*

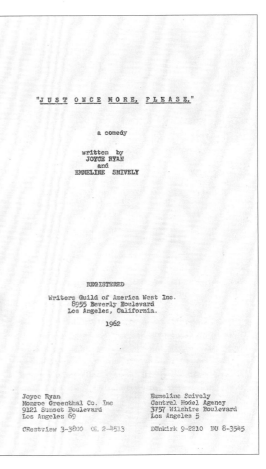

"JUST ONCE MORE, PLEASE."

a comedy

written by
JOYCE RYAN
and
EMMELINE SNIVELY

REGISTERED

Writers Guild of America West Inc.
8955 Beverly Boulevard
Los Angeles, California.

1962

Joyce Ryan
Monroe Greenthal Co. Inc
9121 Sunset Boulevard
Los Angeles 69

CRestview 3-3800 OL 2-4513

Emmeline Snively
Central Model Agency
3757 Wilshire Boulevard
Los Angeles 5

DUnkirk 9-2210 DU 8-3545

and beauty of the agency's members. The furniture consists of two desks, each bearing a telephone, a circular seat (centre stage), a large wall mirror with a six inch high platform before it, a four drawer letter file and several canvas collapsible officer's chairs.

Down front, on the stage, is a trap door which leads to the dark room in the basement. The photographic studio is indicated off stage by spotlights protruding over the top of the partition. The set may be termed artistic but a little home-made.

In the script, mention is made of many of the people Miss Snively and Joyce had worked with during their careers, and they are also given roles in the story. Earl Moran became Albert Weston: 'I had Albert Weston, the artist on the phone,' says Gale. 'He wants a new model for a series of calendars he is painting.' Two models then begin a conversation, which ends with one of them worrying she doesn't have a bathing suit to pose in. 'You don't need a bathing suit,' replies her friend, 'he paints them on.'

Members of the amateur Group 13 photographers club also inspired characters in the script, including Dr Phil Sampson, who became Dr Lampson. Dan Hickson became Sam Dickson, William Gilbert became Billy Gilberts and Richard Whiteman became merely Whiteman.

Miss Snively and Joyce were exceptionally proud of their achievements with the story and wanted to make it into a fully fledged play. Not only that but they wished for Marilyn Monroe and Jayne Mansfield to take on the main roles of Gale Roberts and Jane Smith. 'Both of these girls have similarities,' Miss Snively later wrote. 'Each has great enthusiasm, a sunny, open disposition and the same great interest in people. They also have something else that many a beautiful girl who has come to me lacked and therefore fell by the wayside – persistence. They never gave up.'

Blue Book advert. (From the archive of Ben and Astrid Franse)

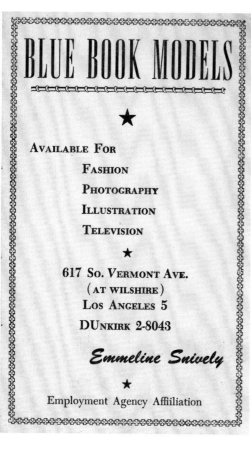

BLUE BOOK MODELS

★

AVAILABLE FOR

FASHION

PHOTOGRAPHY

ILLUSTRATION

TELEVISION

★

617 SO. VERMONT AVE.
(AT WILSHIRE)
LOS ANGELES 5
DUNKIRK 2-8043

Emmeline Snively

★

Employment Agency Affiliation

The part of Gale Roberts was described in the script as 'formerly a model, [she] inherited a little money and decided to open a model agency'. Jane, meanwhile, is a woman who 'invested some of her savings collected by teaching art in high school for a few years'. It is easy to see that Jane is based on Miss Snively, while Gale must be Joyce Ryan. In the script, the agency boss describes herself as 'medium height and colouring, brisk and business-like. She prefers suits although is definitely feminine. All her time and effort is devoted to making the business successful.'

'She prefers suits although is definitely feminine'

Together the women are labelled as: 'ambitious and hard working. They realize the time it takes to build a business handling people and contacts and are trying to establish themselves before their money gives out. They realize the responsibility of guiding and helping young people who are trying to launch themselves in the photographic and motion picture world. Although they are serious about their work, they have a sense of humour which saves them from many a near catastrophe.'

'Marilyn's Final Pose', an article by Louis Sobel from the New York Journal American, 16 August 1962. (From the archive of Ben and Astrid Franse)

Miss Snively wrote to Marilyn again, and while she had been unable to elicit a response from her back in 1958, this time she was in luck. The actress was looking forward to taking a new direction after finishing her latest movie for Twentieth Century Fox, and, after reading the letter, she surprised everyone by contacting the Blue Book office. When the two women spoke, Miss Snively was thrilled to hear that the actress really wanted to see the play. The agency boss wrote about this time in the archive: 'The play was about a struggling model and Marilyn was interested in reading and possibly doing it on the stage. The calls increased during the summer of 1962. Marilyn liked the play. She wanted to [interest] a studio and [thought] maybe the stage had something to offer.'

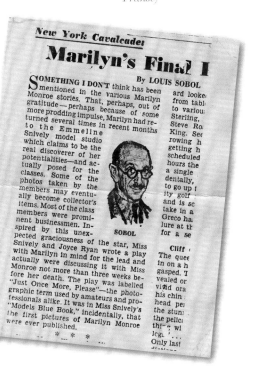

In an article from *Screen Stories* during 1962, the project received a small mention in the gossip section. It read: 'Marilyn Monroe's old friend, Emmeline Snively of the Blue Book Modelling Agency, is writing a play about Marilyn, in collaboration with Joyce Ryan. It's called *Just Once More, Please!* And if that sounds familiar, it's what photographers are always telling their models.'

Shortly after Marilyn's death, journalist Louis Sobel mentioned it in his 16 August 1962 column for the New York Journal America newspaper: 'Miss Snively and Joyce Ryan wrote a play with Marilyn in mind for the lead and actually were discussing it with Miss Monroe not more than three weeks before her death. The play was labelled *Just Once More, Please* – the photographic term used by amateurs and professionals alike.'

* * *

By summer 1962, Marilyn was at a professional standstill, thanks in part to being fired from the set of *Something's Got To Give*. She had lost many

Marilyn takes part in a charity event at Dodger Stadium on her 36th birthday. Unknown photographer. (From the collection of Melinda Mason)

days due to illness, and travelling to New York to sing for President John F. Kennedy was the last straw for the studio. While she had already cleared it with them to go, by the time the date came they refused to let her leave because of the amount of time needed to get her movie back on track. Marilyn went anyway and then called in sick shortly afterwards, which just added to the executives' anger. On the day of her 36th birthday she left the studio for the last time and appeared at a charity baseball game at Dodger Stadium. It was to be the last official public appearance she ever gave.

With no studio work to do, Marilyn dove headlong into a variety of interviews and photo shoots. Perhaps the most famous of which were the sessions with photographer George Barris, during which he took some beautiful shots of her on the beach, wearing a Mexican cardigan. Bert Stern also photographed her, this time in a studio setting, modelling numerous items of clothing; he also took some discreet nudes. However, several other photo sessions have remained a secret, until now.

'It was to be the last official public appearance she ever gave'

The Blue Book Agency was still involved with amateur photographers, who would call on their models to pose in exchange for photos and experience. Extraordinarily, just as she had done during the river session in 1946, it would seem that Marilyn made herself available to pose for the group.

Miss Snively noted in her files that the former model sat for the club members during early summer 1962, though unfortunately she does not elaborate on any other details. However, in amongst all the papers and clippings in the archive is an article by Louis Sobel, who reported on the amateur photo session in his 16 August 1962 column:

> Perhaps out of gratitude – perhaps because of some more prodding impulse, Marilyn had returned several times in recent months to the Emmeline Snively model studio which claims to be the real discoverer of her potentialities, and actually posed for the classes. Some of the photos taken by the members may eventually become collector's items. Most of the class members were prominent businessmen.

The columnist then described the move as being 'unexpected graciousness' on Marilyn's part.

Unfortunately, despite numerous attempts to find these rare and 'new' photographs, the authors have been unable to make contact with any of the businessmen who could have worked with Marilyn during her last summer. Nonetheless, it is hoped that after reading this book, someone, somewhere will recognise the session, check their attics and a new portfolio of photographs will be revealed.

EIGHT

AND SO IT WAS

During the summer of 1962, Marilyn was very much in contact with Miss Snively and Joyce Ryan. All three women were keen to take the play further, and the actress gave some clear indications that she would be more than willing to act in it. The script was not a masterpiece, it should be said, and certainly reading it today shows it to be frightfully dated. However, it is easy to see why Marilyn would be interested in working on it during 1962. Firstly, because the story was based on the life and times of her old model agency, it probably gave her a certain kind of nostalgic feeling. Secondly, if it had been produced for the stage, the project would have given her the opportunity of treading the boards for the first time as a fully fledged star. Aside from that, Marilyn also enjoyed the experience of visiting Blue Book once again, and notes in the archive show that her calls definitely increased during the last summer of her life.

Things had come full circle for Marilyn. Seventeen years after first walking into the Blue Book Agency, she had reacquainted herself with Miss Snively and the two were quietly working together again. The actress had bought a Spanish-style home in the heart of Brentwood, and things seemed more positive and exciting than they had been of late. Sadly this happy time was brief and ended as quickly as it began. On 5 August 1962 Marilyn was found dead in her bedroom, the victim of an apparent overdose. The world mourned the passing of an actress, while many others – including Miss Snively – grieved for the loss of a dear friend. The agency boss wrote about the days that followed in the archive:

> An early morning phone call brings news of Marilyn's death. The next seventy-two hours are a series of phone calls and intrusions, all searching for the same answer, 'Why at thirty-six would Marilyn Monroe take her own life?' At the time of her death Marilyn had no contract with a studio, no husband to call, no home to call so Miss Snively rushed and got Joyce Ryan to help her answer the phones, and dictated to newsmen all over the country.

When Miss Snively heard that Marilyn's room had been found to contain items such as letters, documents and scripts, she immediately began to wonder. She revealed in her notes her belief that the script was one of the items that littered the floor on the night of Marilyn's death. The actress had been found with a telephone in her hand, and, in common with many of Marilyn's friends, Miss Snively prophesised that the unanswered call could have been to her. She was never to find out the answer.

The day after Marilyn's death, journalist Ted Thackrey paid Miss Snively a visit at her office, in order to write an article for the *Los Angeles Herald Examiner* 7 August 1962 edition. The agency boss pulled out the file she kept on Marilyn's career and showed the reporter the name – Norma Jeane – printed on the front, stating that this is what she had always called her. 'But maybe she was really

'maybe she was really Marilyn Monroe – inside – all that time'

Marilyn Monroe – inside – all that time. I don't know.'

On reading her quotes today, it becomes apparent that it was just too soon for Miss Snively to talk about Marilyn, and her shock is scattered throughout the article. She rambled her way through the interview and seemed to forget her train of thought several times. At one point she even told Thackrey that Norma Jeane dyed her hair as soon as she was asked to, which went against everything that she had said prior to and after the interview.

When talking about how hard the model had worked during her time with the agency, Miss Snively sadly stated that everyone should have known just how much Norma Jeane was looking for love, 'not just a job'. Remembering what it was like after Marilyn left Blue Book, the agency boss added that it was only then she realised how scared Norma Jeane had been, and by that point it was too late. 'It was always a little too late for her. A little too late.'

Business card for the Blue Book Model Studio. (From the archive of Ben and Astrid Franse)

An interesting part of the article was when Thackrey asked Miss Snively about the last time she had seen her former student. The agency boss replied that it had been on the set of *There's No Business Like Show Business*. This was not true, of course, as she would later document in her own notes and letters. Perhaps the reason behind not telling the interviewer about the script and renewed friendship was two-fold: it was too soon to get into a big discussion about recent events and, more importantly, she wanted to document the meetings in her own words and in her own projects.

'It was always a little too late for her. A little too late'

One thing Miss Snively did admit to, however, was exactly how she felt about the heartbreak of Marilyn's passing. 'Norma Jeane Dougherty is dead and there are a lot of words and they don't mean anything ... So there's nothing to say ... Nothing to do except look at the pictures and remember a scared, pretty, lonely little kid.' Thackrey asked if she had cried for her former pupil.

'No,' replied Miss Snively. 'It hurts too bad for that.'

* * *

There is some debate over whether or not Miss Snively went to Marilyn's funeral, which was a strictly invitation-only event, organised by the actress's ex-husband and great love, Joe DiMaggio. Her name does not appear on the guest list, but on some of the photos there is a lady which some say could be the agency boss, paying her last respects. In the archive, there is no mention of Miss Snively being at the funeral at all. However, in a note made about an interview she gave to host Charles Collingwood it seems to imply that she was not in attendance:

> Miss Snively wore a wool long-sleeved dress knowing the T.V. would be shown in the winter. It was sweltering under the hot lights and in the summer. Other girls that attended Blue Book because of it having started Marilyn Monroe, came walking in, in their posh dresses and shoes, and stocking footed, having been to the funeral (not invited).

It is not entirely clear as to whether or not Miss Snively was talking about the girls not being invited or herself. However, since she was being interviewed for a television show when the young women returned from observing the funeral, it would seem it is the latter. She continued talking about the television appearance in several other notes:

> Miss Snively put on a cooler dress and her glasses to read a 'cute' letter from MM (when she was getting her divorce from Dougherty), to Mr Collingwood. It was about meeting a movie troupe including Roy Rogers and Trigger, and outsiders thought she was in movies too.

During the interview, the agency boss talked about what it was like to meet Marilyn for the first time and the work she did during her time as a Blue Book model. She then organised photographs to be taken for her files – one of which shows Miss Snively talking to Charles Collingwood, looking at a photograph of Marilyn in her Blue Book directory, with the signed photograph of the star displayed proudly behind her. A cameraman is nearby and a rather glamorous reporter makes notes while sitting on the sofa.

Opposite: Miss Snively's notes about her television appearance, which she made after Marilyn passed away. (From the archive of Ben and Astrid Franse)

NUMBER   PAGE

DATE Aug 4 - 1962   LOCATION
                       Bob Earle Studio - Blue Book Model School

EVENT Marilyns Funeral in Westwood
        Person to Person a flexible Show on Channel #2

OTHER PEOPLE Charles Collingwood - for TV later he called
                                                many -
            Marilyn Manning (Model) Brunette - to keep
                                              Record of Shots

PHOTOGRAPHER Bob Earle Photo   no Release

Comments Miss Snively wore a wool - long sleeved
dress knowing that TV would be shown in the winter
It was sweltering under the hot lights + in the
summer
       Other girls that attended Blue Book because of its ---

in having started M.M. came walking in - in their black
shoes in hand - + stocking footed having been to   dress
the funeral - (not invited) 10 long blocks away.
One had come out on the bus from Ohio (her
home town) + was the first one to call Miss
Snively + break the bad news - Clocks being several
hours earlier there in Ohio.
        After that first call the phones never stopped
ringing.
              At this time of her death Marilyn had no
                    ① Contract with a studio
                    ② husband to call
                    ③ Home to call
                    So Miss Snively Rushed + got
              Joyce Ryan to help her answer the
              Phones - + dictated to ⅗ newsmen
                    all over the country.

NUMBER   PAGE

DATE 1962 Aug 4   LOCATION
                       Blue Book Model School.

EVENT Date Of Funeral of M.M. in Westwood -
She lived not far from the studio

OTHER PEOPLE
        Charles Collingwood

PHOTOGRAPHER Bob Earle (gr 5-3324) Release

Comments Miss Snively put on a cooler dress + her
glasses to read a "cute" letter from M.M. (when she
was getting her divorce in Reno) to Mr Collingwood
It was about meeting a movie troupe including Roy
Rogers + Trigger + outsiders thought she was in movies too!

A more informal shot shows Miss Snively chatting to Collingwood while the female journalist smokes a cigarette. Yet another has the agency boss with a rather shocked look on her face while being questioned by a blonde reporter. Perhaps the most interesting shot taken that day, was the one of Miss Snively reading the letter from Norma Jeane. Tucked away behind Collingwood, but just in view, is the statue of Nefertiti that she had kept on her desk since the days when Norma Jeane was signed to the agency. The model must have seen this ornament many times when she skipped happily into Miss Snively's office, and it surely brought back memories for the agency director.

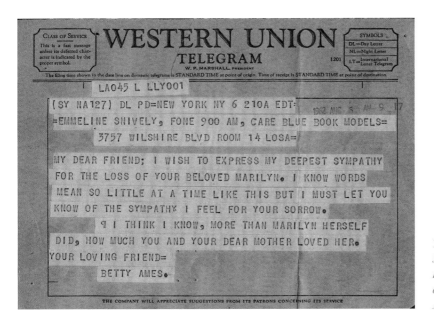

CLASS OF SERVICE

This is a fast message unless its deferred character is indicated by the proper symbol.

WESTERN UNION
TELEGRAM
W. P. MARSHALL, PRESIDENT

1201

SYMBOLS
DL=Day Letter
NL=Night Letter
LT=International Letter Telegram

The filing time shown in the date line on domestic telegrams is STANDARD TIME at point of origin. Time of receipt is STANDARD TIME at point of destination

LA045 L LLY001

(SY NA127) DL PD=NEW YORK NY 6 210A EDT=   1962 AUG 6 AM 9 17

=EMMELINE SNIVELY, FONE 900 AM, CARE BLUE BOOK MODELS=

3757 WILSHIRE BLVD ROOM 14 LOSA=

MY DEAR FRIEND; I WISH TO EXPRESS MY DEEPEST SYMPATHY
FOR THE LOSS OF YOUR BELOVED MARILYN. I KNOW WORDS
MEAN SO LITTLE AT A TIME LIKE THIS BUT I MUST LET YOU
KNOW OF THE SYMPATHY I FEEL FOR YOUR SORROW.
¶ I THINK I KNOW, MORE THAN MARILYN HERSELF
DID, HOW MUCH YOU AND YOUR DEAR MOTHER LOVED HER.
YOUR LOVING FRIEND=
BETTY AMES.

THE COMPANY WILL APPRECIATE SUGGESTIONS FROM ITS PATRONS CONCERNING ITS SERVICE

Telegram to Miss Snively from her friend Betty Ames. (From the archive of Ben and Astrid Franse)

In the days and weeks following Marilyn's death, friends began phoning and visiting the agency to offer their commiserations for the loss of Miss Snively's protégée. Among the correspondence kept over the years was a heart-felt telegram from her friend Betty Ames:

My dear friend, I wish to express my deepest sympathy for the loss of your beloved Marilyn. I know words mean so little at a time like this but I must let you know of the sympathy I feel for your sorrow. I think I know, more than Marilyn herself did, how much you and your dear mother loved her. Your loving friend, Betty Ames.

* * *

Despite Marilyn's death, Miss Snively was determined that her quest to make *Just Once More, Please* should not be abandoned. The actress had expressed her view that it might actually make a good film, and she had offered to show it to several of her contacts. With that in mind, on 10 September 1962, Miss Snively sat down to write a letter to Richard Zanuck of 20th Century Fox, the son of Marilyn's boss, Darryl:

Sept. 10, 1962

Mr. Richard Zanuck
10201 West Pico
Los Angeles, Calif.

Dear Mr. Zanuck:

Enclosed find herewith a film clip on
Norma Jean Dougherty taken from a test
made in 1946 of eight Blue Book model
students in color. This is the first
film done on Norma Jean Dougherty, later
to be known as Marilyn Monroe.

I also have a collection of 8x10 black
and white stills shot from 1945 through
1947. Also a collection of photo
modeling brochures and magazine covers.

During my close association with Marilyn
I met her mother and her Aunt Anna with
whom she lived. I have a charming letter
from Marilyn written to me from Las Vegas
during her first divorce.

I read that you will be doing the Marilyn
Monroe story and wonder if there is a
possibility of my being included in an
advisory capacity during her modeling
years.

*Miss Snively's letter
to Richard Zanuck at
Twentieth Century Fox.
(From the archive of Ben
and Astrid Franse)*

Page 2

Enclosed find Louis Sobol clipping
referring to a script written by Joyce
Ryan and myself. Several years ago
MacKinley Kanter visited my agency and
photographic studio - in fact one of the
members of the photographic class brought
him in. He thought the material too good
to go to waste and that is why we wrote
the script. We believe it to fresh and
different background and are hoping to
do something with it.

Please note page 134 of the Blue Book
Model Directory enclosed.

Sincerely yours,

Emmeline Snively

In connection with Marilyn Monroe I have
been written up in the following:
PEOPLE (see enclosed)
TIME - May 14, 1956, Page 79
TELL IT TO LUELLA
MAURICE ZOLOTOW'S book
McCALLS MAGAZINE - serialized version of
Zolotow's book
THE FIFTY YEAR DECLINE & FALL OF HOLLYWOOD
..by Ezra Goodman.

Dear Mr Zanuck

Please find herewith a film clip on Norma Jeane Dougherty taken from a test made in 1946 of eight Blue Book model students in colour. This is the first film done on Norma Jeane Dougherty, later known as Marilyn Monroe.

I also have a collection of 8 x 10 black and white stills shot from 1945 through 1947. Also a collection of photo modelling brochures and magazine covers.

During my close association with Marilyn I met her mother and her Aunt Ana with whom she lived. I have a charming letter from Marilyn written to me from Las Vegas during her first divorce. I read that you will be doing the Marilyn Monroe story and wonder if there is a possibility of me being included in an advisory capacity during her modelling years.

Enclosed find a Louis Sobel clipping referring to a script written by Joyce Ryan and myself. Several years ago MacKinley Kanter visited my agency and photographic studio – in fact one of the members of the photographic class brought him in. He thought the material too good to go to waste and that is why we wrote the script. We believe it to be fresh and [gives a] different background and are hoping to do something with it.

Please note page 138 of the Blue Book Model Directory enclosed.

Sincerely yours, Emmeline Snively.

Four days later the agency boss received a reply from Mr Zanuck, though it wasn't quite what she expected. Limited to just two sentences, he thanked her for sending the letter but gave assurance that at that moment in time they had no need for the material. Shortly afterwards Miss Snively and Joyce wrote to author and director Abe Burrows, who said the project sounded 'most interesting' but he was not able to commit to working on it. Next was columnist Mike Connolly, who told them that he too was busy, though he did put them in touch with Jule Stein, a songwriter who had worked with Marilyn on *Gentlemen Prefer Blondes*. He was interested in seeing the script, but the women were not so sure, as Joyce later wrote to friend Leon Lance: 'Perhaps we made a mistake, we don't know, but we didn't do it.

E.S.

3757 Wilshire Blvd.
Los Angeles 5, California

December 29, 1962

Mr. Leon Lance
8820 Sunset Blvd.
Los Angeles 69, California.

Dear Leon:

Emmeline and I were happy to talk to you recently when you returned from New York -- hope your cold is better by now - I guess it makes you appreciate California more than ever.

To save us a lot of talking when we get together and so that you may know the background and steps that have been taken so far on our play, "JUST ONCE MORE PLEASE," I am enclosing a copy of a letter we sent to Abe Burrows -- you know he has "HOW TO SUCCEE IN BUSINESS WITHOUT REALLY TRYING" - the biggest smash on Broadway in which your friend and mine, Rudy Vallee has a hit part.   As I heard from him recently, I am enclosing a current letter he sent me which is self-explanatory. I told Rudy you thought well of hi d had his photograph on your office wall. I bought book, "MY TIME IS YOUR TIME", by the way, and it interesting reading.

Abe Burrows wrote us a charming letter saying material sounded most interesting, but he was so ved in his own projects he couldn't contemplate ing else.

saw and talked to Mike Connolly in October said he would be interested in working with he was swamped grinding out his daily column dn't - he loved the title and could catch the vor very readily. He phoned Jule Styne sic for "GENTLEMEN PREFER BLONDES" and t "GYPSY") and made an appointment Y

Leon Lance
- 2 -

for that very afternoon. We hot footed it out to the Beverly Hills Hotel -- and we told him approimately what is contained in the Abe Burrows letter -- and added incidents (he had worked with Marilyn Monroe in "GENTLEMEN PREFER BLONDES". Anyway out "short" interview went into one and a half hours -- he was interested and wanted us to send him a script. Perhaps we made a mistake, we don't know, but we didn't do it -- we felt he was so xbusy on so many things that the script might lie on the bottom of the pile.

I told Mike I would like to meet Ross Hunter at Universal (he has had such comedy hits as "Pillow Talk" etc.) -- Mike said he would introduce us -- so far it has not happened -- I feel he would be good for us, but who knows?

Now it has occured to us too, that Jerry Lewis who has his restaurant on our old location might like the material -- the part of the photographer could be built up for his talents. It is a thought.

Incidentally, Leon, our real life landlord at that ti was Bernard Gionni of the Bank of America. In our p we make the landlord the fellow who owned the resta next door, "Bublichki" -- you probably remember th rotund owner from days of old.

MacKinlay Kantor we are currently corresponding he is going to do "Andersonville" for the screen busy at his home in Sarasota, Florida.

It sounds as if the script has been shopped a actually, this is not true, we have talked ab mentioned here but have been cautious about into the right hands. If you like our mate you would be good for us as you have the p connection and know the field.

Leon Lance
- 3 -

It would be one for the books if after all the years we have known each other something profitable and beneficial could emerge for all of us.

On the other hand, justbecause we have known each other for years, should not make any difference if you find this type of thing is not up your alley. Everyone has told us it is timely and "it isn't what you know but who you know" -- of course, there is something to this -- and we all know more than the average person who just comes to Hollywood - we hope so, anyway.

Please Leon, go over this enclosed material and let us know when we may see you.

Sincerely,

Joyce Ryan
Home: OLYMPIC 2-4513

Emmeline Snively
DUNKIRK 9 - 2210.

The only thing I would really like returned to me is the current letter from Rudy. You can write me at 3757 Wilshire -- I have been working part time with Emmy.

Joyce and Emmeline's letter to friend Leon Lance, describing their play, Just Once More, Please. *(From the archive of Ben and Astrid Franse)*

We felt he was so busy on so many things that the script might lie on the bottom of the pile.'

The search for a suitable partner did not stop there. The women decided that actor Jerry Lewis would be good for the role of a photographer in the play, and they thought it was a great coincidence that he now owned a restaurant in the old location of the agency. As luck would have it, a charity Lewis was working for asked the agency for a model to pose with him. Joyce later wrote about what happened next, in a letter to Mike Connolly:

> Emmeline went to the photographic studio at Paramount the day of the shooting, hoping to meet Jerry Lewis. He was two hours late so she had to leave. In the meantime she met Hal Bell who works with Lewis, who promised to put our letter on Lewis' desk. So there you are! You can see we can't handle this in the proper way!

Eventually, despite all the efforts of both Miss Snively and Joyce to get the script into the right hands, their plans fell through. While people were positive about the project, nobody was able or interested enough to get involved. The two women still believed in the script, but with Marilyn gone, and nobody else prepared to commit, they knew it was hopeless. The project was shelved and the two turned their attentions to another plan, which would turn into the last thing Miss Snively would ever do in connection with Marilyn and her agency.

Miss Snively and Joyce created lists of pictures, photographers, phone numbers, notes, memories and much more, all related to Blue Book's most famous model. Finally they felt ready and in 1969 Miss Snively asked Joyce to write a passionate letter to prospective publishers:

Chapter titles for the book Miss Snively and Joyce wanted to write about Marilyn (many of which have been incorporated into this book). (From the archive of Ben and Astrid Franse)

Dear Sir

I am currently in the process of writing a book on the career of Marilyn Monroe between 1946 and 1950. As my associates in this effort I have two people closely connected with her during this period: Emmeline Snively, agent, modelling instructor and close friend of Norma Jeane Dougherty (Marilyn Monroe) and Earl Moran, calendar artist and prior employer of Norma Jeane from 1946–1949. Mr Moran used Marilyn as a model for many of his calendars in oil. In addition to these memories we are including letters, telegrams and over three hundred (mostly unpublished) photographs from this same time span. (In addition to the photographs we plan to use, there are about twenty unpublished nude photographs of Marilyn. A decision on whether or not to use these photographs will be made when we have a publisher – based on the publisher's policies and views).

Due to the large number of photographs I am attempting to hold the story at under 40,000 words. However, I am willing to expand or contract the story to suit the publisher.

Attached is an outline of the story. At this time four chapters are complete and I will forward you copies if you are interested. If you would like to see part or all of the photographs I will bring them to New York at your request, if a definite appointment is made with one of your representatives. I will take care of my own expenses but I will not mail or leave the photographs without a definite contract. We have releases on all of the photographs we plan to include in the publication. Our present selection for a title is *And so it was* but we are willing to discuss changes.

While the book is an effort on the part of Miss Snively, Mr Moran and myself, I will handle all contract negotiations.

Even though Marilyn has been dead for over seven years I believe that a book on this span in her career is marketable. Some sources state that Marilyn has more fans today than she did at the time of her death. The publication by _____ Norma Jeane by _____ seems to indicate that the subject is still saleable. The collections of photographs alone should make this book a must for all Marilyn Monroe followers.

Dear Sir,

I am currently in the process of writing a book on the career of Marilyn Monroe between 1946 and 1950. As my associates in this effort I have two people closely connected with her during that period: Emmeline Snively, agent, modeling instructor and close friend of Norma Jean Dougherty (Marilyn Monroe) and Earl Moran, calendar artist and prime employer of Norma Jean from 1945-1949. In addition to their memories we are including letters, telegrams and over 300 (mostly unpublished) photographs from this same time span. (In addition to the photographs we plan to use, there are about 20 unpublished nude photographs of Marilyn. A decision on whether or not to use these photographs will be made—when we have a publisher—based on the publication and views.)

Due to the large number of photographs I am attempting to hold the story at under 40,000. However, I am willing to expand or contract the story to suit a publisher.

2) Attached is an outline of the story. At this time, four chapters are complete and I will forward you copies if you are interested. If you would like to see part or all of the photographs I will bring them to New York at your request, if a definite appointment is made with one of your representatives. I will take care of my own expenses but I will not mail or leave the photographs without a definite contract. We have release on all of the photographs we plan to include in the publication. Our present selection for a title is "And So It Was" but we are willing to discuss changes.

While the book is an effort on the part of Miss Snively and myself, I will handle all the Moran contract negotiations—

3) Even tho Marilyn has been dead for over 7 years I believe that a book on this span in her career is marketable. Some sources state that Marilyn has more fans today than she did at the time of her death. The publication by Norma Jean is still salable. (my own) The collection of photographs alone should make the book a must for all Marilyn Monroe followers.

Thank you for your time and consideration and I hope to hear from you in the near future.

Sincerely,
Joyce

Joyce's letter to prospective publishers outlining her and Miss Snively's book about Marilyn. (From the archive of Ben and Astrid Franse)

Thank you for your time and consideration. I hope to hear from you in the near future.

Sincerely

Joyce Ryan

* * *

In the end, despite her enthusiasm and commitment, none of Miss Snively's plans came to fruition. She and Joyce sent the sample chapters to various publishers but nobody wanted to produce the book. It was still a relatively short time since Marilyn died, and companies felt there was no call for a volume about her modelling career. The 1960s reached out towards the 1970s, and Miss Snively knew that time was running out. Her health was beginning to fail, and the rejection of the Marilyn book was the last straw. She took the difficult decision to retire from the modelling business and sold many of her photographs to magazines around the country. Eventually she gathered up the remainder of her photos, along with the Marilyn files, and put them all in a box, where no doubt she thought they would remain forever. One of the last things she ever wrote is reproduced here:

The days of the glamour girl are fading and many of the magazines Marilyn appeared on have ceased to exist. The Spanish house still stands – acquired by a pleasant middle aged couple. They are haunted by the curious who still come to see where the legend had died. The cemetery hidden a few feet from busy Wilshire Boulevard is visited only occasionally nowadays. Joe DiMaggio visits once in a while and the red roses he sends always are on the crypt.

The Casino floor office at the Ambassador is now part of the post office. The back lots of Twentieth Century Fox are now a development. Earl Moran lives quietly and continues to paint nudes in oil. The trees on the Tujunga River were washed away in the floods a few years ago and as one looks at the changes today, you can still look back to the girl who became a legend.

And so it was …

Chapter 1 - Sunday, August 5, 1962 - An early morning phone call bring news of Marilyn's death. The next 72 hours are a series of phone calls and interviews all searching for the same answer. "Why at 36 would Marilyn Monroe take her own life?" Since Marilyn was at this time not assigned to any studio many of the news men and friends of Marilyn contacted Miss Snively for the answer to these questions.

Notes for Chapter One of Emmeline's book. (From the archive of Ben and Astrid Franse)

Notes for Chapter 5. (From the archive of Ben and Astrid Franse)

Chapter 5 - "Cross my heart I die" Norma Jean went to Reno to obtain her divorce. This was a lonely point in her life. Norma Jean had very few friends. She was always friendly with the other models and the photographers but she never went out socially with them. Miss Snively became more than an employer - Norma Jean felt she could trust and confide in her. During the six week waiting period Miss Snively received many ten stamped letters. However, the one she remembers but was written during one of the puppy mommy be made a ... Norma Jean had gone to watch the shooting. The crew was as attracted to the beautiful girl as she to them. The models... her to have lunch with them and she met Roy Rogan. Norma loved horses and was more attracted to trigger than Roy Rogan. She was allowed to ride

With the agency no longer active, Miss Snively moved to Huntingdon beach, where she occasionally spent time with friends Joyce Ryan and Joyce Black. Her days of power and fame were behind her, but she tried to lead an active life, until one day in the early 1970s when she collapsed and fell down the stairs. Doctors diagnosed a stroke, and the previously independent woman was suddenly unable to care for herself any more. Life was never the same again for Miss Snively, and she was forced to move in with friends for a time, before it was discovered that she had cancer and needed more specialist care.

Moving into the Huntingdon Valley Convalescent Hospital, Miss Snively withdrew into herself. At the height of her career she had always dressed immaculately, spoke passionately to guests and wore a classy hat on her head. Now, within the confines of the hospital, she covered her grey hair with a scarf and received few visitors.

Two of the last people to see Miss Snively alive were distant cousins Beverly and Paul. Paul had been represented by the Blue Book Agency for a time, and it would be easy to imagine that much of what he spoke about revolved around the days he had spent there. Miss Snively sat quietly, lost it seems in her own foggy recollections. The woman who had reigned over one of the busiest West Coast agencies was now incredibly lonely. Her memories – once as bright as the beaming illuminations on Hollywood Boulevard – were now tiny shards of light, dimming quietly and fading away into the darkness of the night.

On 17 September 1975, Miss Snively suffered a last stroke, which sadly claimed her life at the age of just 66. Morna Flick, a distant relative, informed the necessary authorities and ordered the death certificate. The funeral took place at Loma Vista Memorial Park just two days later, on 19 September 1975.

In life she had discovered many models and launched the careers of Marilyn Monroe and Jayne Mansfield. From the 1930s onwards, her office was inundated with thousands of amateur starlets, all wishing to get their big break in Hollywood. Called upon frequently to talk about Marilyn in print and on television, Miss Snively was a popular woman, but on that sad day in mid September, it was as though she had never existed at all.

Not one person attended her memorial service. Not one.

Nobody stood in the chapel and spoke animatedly about her days in Hollywood. Nobody declared their love or expressed how much Miss Snively had changed their lives. Nobody laid flowers or wept at her passing. Instead she was quietly cremated without fanfare or flourish, and no one claimed the expense bill or picked up her ashes from the memorial park. Her distant cousins were not told of her death until months later, and by that time it was too late to attend the funeral or pay their respects.

Miss Snively, the ambitious manager of the Blue Book Model Agency, died a deserted woman, her days of glamour and beauty long behind her. Like Marilyn, she lived a busy life and made history several times over, but in the end – just like her pupil – she died alone. However, Marilyn had former husband Joe DiMaggio to claim her body and organise her funeral; Miss Snively, on the other hand, had no one.

(From the archive of Ben and Astrid Franse)

As a result of this deeply sad ending, her ashes are now kept in a plastic container within a special storage facility. They have remained unclaimed and seemingly unwanted for the past forty years. In tribute to her, therefore, it seems fitting that the last words in this book be hers:

Students who know that Marilyn Monroe is my prize graduate occasionally ask me if there is any possibility of their 'getting the same breaks Marilyn Monroe got.' My answer to that one is, 'What breaks?' Marilyn Monroe, I tell them, is a self-made success. Of course, she's endowed with charm, personality and a provocative figure, but thousands of girls are similarly endowed. What most of them lack Marilyn has in spades – persistence and fortitude. These are two requisites for any person who wants to crash Hollywood. This is no town for the weak, the weary or the easily-defeated.

Emmeline Snively, 1954

For Twenty-Three years Blue Book Models have been known around the world. The high degree of success enjoyed by Blue Book Models has been due to the best touch of Miss Emmeline Snively. Miss Snively has gained National Recognition for discovering, training and promoting new comers in the Modeling and Talent Fields. Jayne Mansfield was given her First Job by Miss Snively and as a result of the training and promotion at Blue Book Models Marilyn Monroe appeared on countless National magazine covers. Marilyn started with Blue Book Models in 1947.

Miss Snively received her B.E. degree in Art and Education at UCLA and continued her graduate work in Art on the Berkly Campus.

Blue Book Model studios are located at 2307 West Wood Blvd in West Los Angeles. All training is conducted under the close supervision of Miss Snively, who teaches certain courses herself. Miss Snively

Miss Snively's biography.
(From the archive of Ben and Astrid Franse)

... Central Model Agency ... Manager 422 South Western ... Los Angeles. It is though ... outlet that Many of the Blue Book Model received their First Jobs and the promotion necessary for success in this highly competitive field.

Miss Snively is the publisher of the Models Blue Book which has become renown as the "who's who" of Hollywood Models. In early 1969 Miss Snively will enter the publishing field with her new Quarterly publication "How to Crash Hollywood" which will be a directory and pointing ...

BIBLIOGRAPHY

Banner, Lois W., *MM — Personal: From the Private Archive of Marilyn Monroe* (Abrams, 2011)

Bernard, Susan, *Bernard of Hollywood's Marilyn* (Boxtree Ltd, 1994)

Bernard, Susan, *Marilyn: Intimate Exposures* (Sterling, 2011)

Comment, Bernard and Buchthal, Stanley, *Fragments: Poems, Intimate Notes, Letters* (HarperCollins, 2010)

De Dienes, Andre, *Marilyn Mon Amour* (Sidgwick and Jackson, 1986)

De Dienes, Andre, *Marilyn* (Taschen, 2011)

Finn, Michelle, *Marilyn's Addresses* (Smith Gryphon, 1995)

Jasgur, Joseph and Sakol, Jeannie, *The Birth of Marilyn* (Sidgwick and Jackson, 1991)

Miracle, Berniece Baker and Miracle, Mona Rae, *My Sister Marilyn* (Algonquin Books, 1994)

Monroe, Marilyn and Hecht, Ben, *My Story* (Taylor Trade Publishing, 2007)

Morgan, Michelle, *Marilyn Monroe: Private and Undisclosed* (Robinson, 2012)

Snively, Emmeline and Ryan, Joyce, *Just Once More, Please* (1962)

Victor, Adam, *The Complete Marilyn Monroe* (Thames and Hudson, 1999)

Wills, David, *Marilyn Monroe: Metamorphosis* (It Books, 2011)

Woodard, Eric with Marshall, David, *Hometown Girl* (HG Press, 2004)